MORE F
M · O ·
COOKBOOK

A Carousel of Thrifty Cooking Ideas

Great American Opportunities, Inc./Favorite Recipes® Press

Published by: Favorite Recipes® Press, a division of Great American Opportunities, Inc.
P. O. Box 305142
Nashville, TN 37230

Printed in the United States of America.

First Printing: 1990

Library of Congress Catalog Number: 89-71439
ISBN: 0-87197-267-0

Preface

Whether the household you manage is just you or a family of ten, you are a manager.

Certainly a big part of being a good manager is getting the most for your food dollar. That's why this book was published — to help you get the most for your food dollar. And to show you how you can have great tasting meals with lots of variety and still stay within a reasonable food budget.

In this book you'll find hundreds of recipes created by thrifty homemakers . . . shopping advice . . . substitutions to stretch your food dollar . . . wonderfully creative ideas for using leftovers . . . great new ways to use your freezer and microwave . . . and many innovative ways of buying and preparing food.

This book's recipes for delicious but low-cost foods and its timesaving ideas are shared with you by homemakers throughout America. These women face the same problem you do — trying to meet a family's nutritional needs without spending more than is budgeted for food. They have hundreds of little tricks to prepare balanced meals at a low cost — and in this book they share those secrets with you.

As you browse through these pages, you'll find yourself becoming excited as you discover ways to cut down on today's high food costs. You'll begin to see how you can actually have money left over after you shop for food — money that can be used to buy the little extras that make life more enjoyable.

Contents

Shopping Hints

GETTING MORE FOR YOUR MONEY

Every week, it seems you spend more money at the grocery store. With your big investment in food, you are naturally concerned about getting the most from every dollar you spend. Here are some tried-and-proven hints to cut down food costs.

Read the food ads. One day each week, all the grocery stores in your area will advertise their specials . . . in most communities these ads appear on Wednesday or Thursday. Take the time to sit down with a heavy marking pencil or crayon and circle the first and second best buys each store is featuring. List these buys and choose your greatest values.

Plan your week's menus. Using the foods that are on special sale as a guide, plan your entire week's menus. Feature dishes using the specials of the week. Take advantage of the seasonal specials, too. In this book we have listed fruits and vegetables by their season to guide you to the best buys.

Make a detailed shopping list. Start by listing all the foods you will need to make the dishes you have indicated on your week's menus. Then check your storage cupboards and refrigerator to see what items you are running low on. Here's a quick trick to cut down the time it usually takes to make a list. When you use an item and notice that you are running low on it, mark the container with a grease pencil. When you are making up your list, all you have to do is write down the items in these marked containers – no more shaking boxes and examining the levels in your bottles.

Eat before you shop. Repeated surveys have indicated that if you are hungry when you shop for food, you may spend six or seven dollars more than if you had shopped after eating. Something about all that food in the store and the gnawing hunger in your stomach leads you to buy more than you intended . . . or needed.

Compare stores. To get the most value for your money, home economists recommend, you need to shop in three to five stores to fulfill your grocery list. By shopping in a number of stores, you can be sure of getting the lowest prices, of finding a large number of different items on "special." There may be some instances when it is not economically feasible to shop in so many stores each week – perhaps you don't have the transportation available. But generally, comparison shopping among different stores pays dividends in the form of food dollars saved.

Compare prices. When considering fresh food, compare the cost *per serving* of fresh versus both frozen and canned. You may actually save money buying frozen or canned vegetables and fruit, especially out of season. Consider, too, the cost per serving of various cuts of meat, poultry, and fish – allow three-quarters of a pound of bone-in and one-half a pound of boneless per serving.

Buy the store brands. A recent Federal Trade Commission survey concluded that prices of store brands average 12 percent lower than precisely the same quality of food sold under established "big brand" names.

Use your shopping list. Most home economists agree that few things can inflate a family's food costs as quickly as "impulse buying" . . . that insidious habit of picking up one of these and a few of those until you have added as much as one-third to your original list. If you really have trouble resisting the extras and keeping to a budget, invest in one of the small pocket calculators. Set a dollar amount as a limit for yourself. Punch in the price of every item you pick up, whether included on your list or not. When you reach your limit, that's it. A few times of returning those expensive extras to the shelves will cure even the most compulsive impulse buyer!

Know what a special is. So far, the specials we have been talking about are "loss leaders" . . . items grocers feature at a loss in profit to attract customers to their stores. But there are several other specials you should know about. One is the quick markdown – a grocer may have too much of an item and want to clear his shelf quickly. Then he usually handwrites a sign and puts it up. These hand-printed signs are often guideposts to great bargains. If a store is out of its special, ask for a "rain check." This is a certificate entitling you to buy an advertised special at sale price when the item is restocked.

Know what you are buying. Take the time to learn what the various gradings of meat, vegetables, and fruits mean. For instance, in vegetable and fruit gradings, Grade A is the extra-fancy quality food usually used in fine restaurants or in dishes where the appearance of the food is important. Grade B is food intended for general use, and Grade C is less fancy food but contains the same nutritional values as Grades A and B. Grades B and C are priced considerably lower than Grade A.

Finally, get to know the people you are dealing with. The store manager who knows you as one of his regular customers will sometimes tell you that an item is about to be put on special – he may even let you buy it a day early! The checker who remembers you from week to week will be extra careful to ring up your order quickly and correctly. And the stock boys will be glad to look in the back room for more cans or boxes of a depleted special. Your grocery store is one of the many places where a smile and a few nice words will pay enormous dividends!

Appetizers, Beverages, & Accompaniments

Appetizers are so versatile! They cover the gamut from tidbits to nibble on before dinner to the entire evening's repast. These recipes are as creative as they are easy with a variety of hot and cold selections. They're made to order for your next party, especially since many can be prepared ahead to help you avoid last minute entertaining panic.

But keep in mind that the way you arrange appetizers is as important as the food itself. Prepare several small dishes which can be easily refilled . . . a large one loses its attractiveness as the evening wears on. Garnish appetizers with parsley, watercress, thin lemon twists, carrot curls or radish roses. Remember — a little color goes a long way!

The beverage recipes in this chapter are as appealing as they are tasty — from frozen malts to peachy punch.

Appetizers, Beverages, & Accompaniments

GETTING MORE FOR YOUR MONEY

GREAT GARNISHES

A little imagination goes a long way toward making your food dishes look as good as they taste!

GARNISHING FOODS

Carrot Curls

Clean and scrape carrot. With a potato peeler, peel down lengthwise into paper-thin slices. Roll up each slice and fasten with a toothpick. Chill in ice water. To decorate, remove toothpicks and, if desired, place a ripe olive in the center of each curl.

Celery Tassels

Cut stalk into 2-inch pieces. Slit at narrow intervals down the length of each piece – almost to the end. Chill in ice water to curl. Use as an edible garnish for dips.

Gherkin Pickle Fans

Drain cocktail gherkins thoroughly. Slice down the length 3 to 4 times almost to the end. Gently spread slices apart to form a fan.

Radish Roses

An inexpensive bright spot of color for open sandwiches, appetizers, meat and vegetables dishes. Make 6 to 8 cuts lengthwise from the base of the radish towards the stalk. Chill in ice water until they open like flowers. If radishes are extra long, cut lengthwise at intervals so they will open up accordian fashion.

Chocolate Leaves

Wash and dry rose leaves. Melt one bag of chocolate chips over boiling water, then beat vigorously until smooth. Run one leaf at a time upside down over the chocolate surface to cover evenly. (To remove any extra chocolate, tap the leaf, against the side of the bowl.) Harden leaf on a cookie sheet, chocolate-side up, in the refrigerator. Peel away the leaves, and you'll have a perfect chocolate leaf.

Chocolate Curls

Pour melted chocolate chips as thinly as possible onto a very cold surface. Marble is best, but if not available, ice down the kitchen counter or table. Let chocolate harden for about two hours or until it has lost its gloss. Hold the knife with both hands at a slight angle and rake across the chocolate surface, using a pivot-like motion. Use these beautiful curls to decorate cakes or other desserts.

Frosted Grapes

Wash grapes thoroughly; dip into slightly beaten egg white, then coat with granulated sugar. Dry on waxed paper and refrigerate until needed.

Spun Sugar

Bring two cups of sugar and one cup of water to a boil. Using a candy thermometer, boil until syrup reaches 312 degrees. Remove from heat and stir in a pinch of cream of tartar. As the syrup cools, it forms fine threads when dropped from a wooden spoon. Holding an oiled spoon horizontally, pass the syrup over the handle twirling the fine threads onto tortes, cookies or cakes.

Mint Leaves

A seasonal delicacy for summer fruit desserts. Select firm, small mint sprigs or individual leaves. Brush lightly with egg white and dredge through superfine sugar. Dry and use the same day.

Chantilly Cream

A beautiful, delicious garnish piped or spooned onto desserts. Whip one cup heavy cream in bowl with an electric mixer until stiff peaks form. Add two tablespoons confectioners' sugar, one tablespoon at a time, beating gently. Add one teaspoon of desired flavoring, a small amount at a time. Fold in one stiffly beaten egg white, gently but thoroughly. Certainly more delicious than plain whipped cream.

GARNISHING BEVERAGES

- Garnish cool drinks with fruit slices cut in wedges or chunks, scoops of sherbet or ice cream, mint sprigs or cucumber slices.
- Add flavor and color to hot, milky drinks with cinnamon sticks, whipped cream or marshmallow creme. For cool drinks, use candy canes or clove-studded lime or lemon slices.
- Hot holiday beverages look pretty garnished with a dab of whipped cream that's topped with a sprinkle of cinnamon, nutmeg or ginger.
- To attractively garnish drinks or punch, place slices of lemon peel or mint leaves in ice cube trays before freezing.
- For colorful cubes, freeze fruit juices in ice trays: orange and pineapple for gin or vodka drinks, tomato juice for Bloody Mary's, or lemon and lime juice for snappier sours.

MAKE SWEET PICKLES FROM DILL PICKLES

Excellent sweet pickles may be made from more inexpensive whole dill pickles. Slice dill pickles into jar. Combine 1 cup dill pickle liquid, 2 cups sugar, 13 whole cloves, 1 tablespoon celery seed and 1 tablespoon mustard seed in saucepan; mix well. Bring mixture to a boil; pour over dill pickles. Seal. Pickles will be ready for use in 2 days. Save liquid for next batch of pickles.

Madalynne McKague
Rochester, New York

APPETIZER HAM BALL

2 4 1/2-oz. cans deviled ham
3 tbsp. chopped stuffed green olives
1 tbsp. prepared mustard
Tabasco sauce to taste
1 3-oz. package cream cheese, softened
2 tsp. milk

Combine ham, olives, mustard and Tabasco sauce; shape into ball on serving dish. Chill. Blend cream cheese and milk; frost ball with mixture. Remove from refrigerator 15 minutes before serving. Garnish with parsley.

Mrs. Johnnie Mae Proctor
Dilley, Texas

CHEESE NACHOS

1 can bean dip
1 pkg. taco chips
Grated Cheddar cheese

Spread a small amount of dip on each taco chip; place on paper plate. Sprinkle with cheese. Microwave on High for 35 seconds or until cheese has melted.

C. Lee
San Francisco, California

CHEESE ROLL

1 8-oz. package Velveeta cheese, softened
8 oz. longhorn Cheddar cheese, shredded
3 cloves of garlic, minced
1 c. chopped pecans
Paprika

Blend cheeses, garlic and pecans together until thoroughly mixed. Roll in paprika until well covered. Serve with crackers.

Mrs. Gayle Foutch
Fort Worth, Texas

DEVILED EGGS

6 hard-cooked eggs, halved lengthwise, yolks removed
2 tbsp. mayonnaise
1/2 tsp. salt
1/4 tsp. pepper
1 tbsp. sweet pickle, chopped
1 tsp. finely chopped onion

Mash egg yolks with fork. Add remaining ingredients; blend well. Fill egg whites. Garnish with sliced stuffed olives, paprika or parsley. Chill. Yield: 6 servings.

Mrs. Anna Marie Acosta
Carencro, Louisiana

HOT ONION APPETIZERS

1/2 c. butter
1/2 pkg. onion soup mix
1 10-count pkg. refrigerator biscuits

Melt butter in electric skillet at 150 degrees. Add soup mix; blend well. Cut biscuits into quarters; place in skillet. Cook, covered, at 275 degrees for 20 minutes or until brown, turning once. Reduce heat to lowest setting; keep warm. Serve hot with toothpicks.

Betty Hagberg
Chisago City, Minnesota

MICROWAVE CHEESY TORTILLA ROLL-UPS

1 1/2 c. shredded sharp Cheddar cheese
3 tbsp. dry onion soup mix
1/2 c. sour cream
1/4 c. Parmesan cheese
12 flour tortillas

Combine Cheddar cheese, soup mix, sour cream and Parmesan cheese; mix well. Spread 3 tablespoons mixture on each tortilla; roll as for jelly roll. Cut each roll-up into 3 pieces; secure with toothpicks. Arrange roll-ups on plate. Microwave on High for 1 minute. Serve immediately. Yield: 3 dozen.

Jeanne Winterfield
Toppenish, Washington

MICROWAVE MEXICALI NACHOS

8 oz. cream cheese, softened
1 16-oz. can chili without beans
1 4-oz. can chopped green chilies
1 sm. green bell pepper, chopped
1 sm. onion, minced
1 c. shredded Cheddar cheese

Spread cream cheese in 8 x 8-inch glass dish. Layer chili, green chilies, green pepper and onion on cream cheese. Microwave on High for 4 minutes. Serve warm with tortilla chips.

Luan Montag
West Bend, Iowa

SAUCY COCKTAIL FRANKS

1 c. red currant jelly
1 tbsp. hot prepared mustard
1 16-oz. package cocktail franks

Melt jelly over medium heat; blend in mustard. Add franks; stir gently until franks are heated through and covered with jelly mixture. Place in server over candle warmer. Serve with toothpicks. Yield: 6-8 servings.

Mrs. Jack E. N. Spratt
Riverside, Connecticut

MICROWAVE TIPS FOR APPETIZERS

You can crisp stale crackers, potato chips and pretzels in the microwave by heating them on High for 15 to 30 seconds. If you forget to take the cheese out of the refrigerator in time to reach room temperature, Microwave it on Medium-High just long enough to remove the chill. Cream cheese for dips and cheese balls can be softened by microwaving on Low for 8 or 9 minutes.

Paula Winfield
Effingham, Illinois

MEATBALL APPETIZERS

1 lb. ground beef
1 tsp. Accent
3/4 tsp. salt
1 tbsp. chopped onion
1/2 c. soft bread crumbs
1/4 c. milk
1 tbsp. flour
2 tbsp. butter
3 tbsp. molasses
3 tbsp. prepared mustard
3 tbsp. vinegar
1/4 c. catsup
1/4 tsp. thyme

Break up meat with fork in mixing bowl. Sprinkle with Accent, salt and onion. Combine bread crumbs and milk in bowl; add to meat mixture. Toss lightly until well blended. Shape into 3/4-inch balls; roll in flour. Brown in butter in skillet. Combine remaining ingredients; blend until smooth. Add to meatballs. Simmer for 8 to 10 minutes or until sauce thickens and meatballs are glazed, stirring occasionally. Serve from chafing dish as hot hors d'oeuvre. Yield: 50 meatballs.

Photograph for this recipe on page 6.

TUNA CANAPES

2 6 1/2-oz. cans tuna in vegetable oil
2 tsp. bleu cheese salad dressing mix
1/2 c. finely chopped celery
1/2 c. mayonnaise
1/2 c. sour cream (opt.)

Combine all ingredients; mix until well blended. Place tuna mixture on toast rounds; broil for 2 to 3 minutes. Yield: 3 dozen canapes.

Cindy Pelham
Corsicana, Texas

CLAM DUNK

1 8-oz. package cream cheese, softened
2 tsp. lemon juice
1 8-oz. can minced clams, drained
2 tsp. chili sauce (opt.)
2 tsp. Worcestershire sauce
1 tsp. salt
1/8 tsp. pepper
Dash of hot pepper sauce
Paprika

Blend cream cheese and lemon juice; add clams and remaining ingredients except paprika, mixing well. Sprinkle with paprika. Chill. Serve with garlic rounds. Yield: 1 1/2 cups.

Shirley J. Bonomo
Spring Valley, Wisconsin

DEVIL'S DIP

1/4 c. sliced mushrooms
1/4 c. chopped celery
1/4 c. chopped onion
3 tbsp. margarine
1 can mushroom soup
1 pkg. frozen chopped broccoli, cooked and drained
1 6-oz. package garlic cheese, cubed
Dash of hot sauce

Saute mushrooms, celery and onion in margarine until soft but not brown; add soup, broccoli and cheese. Cook slowly, stirring constantly, until cheese is melted; add hot sauce. Pour into warm chafing dish. Serve with corn chips. Yield: 10 servings.

Mable Moorhouse
Belen, New Mexico

FIESTA BEAN DIP

2 c. hot cooked pinto beans, mashed
Bean liquid
1 c. grated sharp Cheddar cheese
2 tbsp. minced onion
1 lge. clove of garlic, mashed
1 jalapeno pepper, finely chopped
1 tsp. jalapeno liquid

Combine beans and enough bean liquid to make of dipping consistency in saucepan. Add remaining ingredients; mix well. Cook over low heat until cheese is melted. Serve hot with tortillas or cold as sandwich spread.

Mrs. Thelma McClain
Bremond, Texas

MIDNIGHT DIP

1 can bean with bacon soup
1/4 c. chili sauce
2 tbsp. minced green pepper
1 tsp. minced onion
1 tsp. Worcestershire sauce

Mix all ingredients well. Chill. Yield: 1 1/2 cups.

Carolyn Mullins
Wartrace, Tennessee

NIPPY CHEESE DIP

1 10-oz. package sharp Cheddar cheese, grated
1 tbsp. grated onion

Dash of salt
1 tbsp. Worcestershire sauce
Mayonnaise

Place cheese, onion, salt and Worcestershire sauce in bowl. Add enough mayonnaise for dipping consistency; serve with crackers, stuff celery or use as spread for sandwiches. Store in airtight container in refrigerator.

Mrs. Dorthy G. Wood
Staunton, Virginia

SMOKED EGG DIP

6 hard-cooked eggs, finely chopped
1 tbsp. soft butter
1 1/4 tsp. liquid smoke
1 1/2 tsp. lemon juice
1 tsp. mustard
1 1/2 tsp. Worcestershire sauce
1 drop of hot sauce
3/4 tsp. salt
1/2 tsp. dried minced onions

Combine all ingredients; beat with electric mixer until smooth. Refrigerate for 4 hours. Whip before serving at room temperature.

Mrs. Marilyn B. Hoffman
Oxford, Mississippi

VEGETABLE DIP

1 c. mayonnaise
1 c. catsup
1/3 c. lemon juice
1 tbsp. dry mustard
2 tbsp. horseradish, drained
1 tbsp. sugar
1/2 tsp. Worcestershire sauce
1/4 tsp. pepper
1/2 tsp. salt

Combine all ingredients; mix well. Chill until thickened. May be kept in tightly closed container in refrigerator for several days. Serve with fresh vegetables for dipping. Yield: 2 cups.

Mabel V. Garst
Eaton, Ohio

SPICED PECANS

1 c. sugar
1/2 c. water
1 tsp. cinnamon
1/4 tsp. salt
1 tsp. vanilla
2 1/2 c. whole pecans

Combine all ingredients except vanilla and pecans in saucepan. Cook over medium heat to 232 degrees on candy thermometer. Remove from heat; add vanilla and pecans, stirring until nuts are well coated and mixture is creamy. Pour onto baking sheet. Separate nuts with forks while cooling.

Patricia Irvin
Wells, Minnesota

MEXICAN CHOCOLATE

1/4 lb. sweet chocolate
5 1/2 c. milk
1/2 c. cream
1 tbsp. cinnamon
1/8 tsp. nutmeg
1 tsp. vanilla
8 2 1/2-in. cinnamon sticks

Combine chocolate and 1 cup hot water in top of double boiler; heat until chocolate is melted. Stir. Combine milk, cream, cinnamon and nutmeg in 3-quart saucepan; beat with rotary beater or wire wisk until well blended. Cook, stirring occasionally, over medium heat until bubbles form around edge of pan. Remove from heat. Stir in melted chocolate and vanilla; beat with rotary beater until foamy. Serve with a cinnamon stick in each cup. Yield: 6 servings.

Mrs. Jack O'Neill
Belmont, Wisconsin

HANDY HOMEMADE COCOA MIX

Homemade cocoa mix gives a richer flavor at a lower cost per cup. One pound of mix may be made by sifting 1 1/2 cups cocoa and 1 1/2 cups sugar together. Store in tightly covered container. Use 2 to 3 heaping teaspoons per cup of hot milk to serve.

Evelyn B. Willey
Gatesville, North Carolina

FROZEN CHOCOLATE MALTS

3 c. chilled chocolate milk
1/2 c. malted milk powder
1 qt. vanilla ice cream, cubed
Whipped cream (opt.)

Mix milk, malted milk powder and 1 pint ice cream quickly with hand mixer or in blender until smooth but still thick. Add remaining ice cream; mix quickly. Pour into 4 chilled 10 or 12-ounce glasses. Freeze for 2 to 3 hours or until quite firm. Top with whipped cream; garnish with chocolate curls or crushed peppermint candy. Serve immediately.

Francine Dexter
Broadside, Maryland

COCOA

2 2/3 c. instant nonfat dry milk
7 1/2 c. water
1/2 c. sugar
1/2 c. (or more) chocolate-flavored drink mix

Dissolve dry milk in water in saucepan; mix well. Add sugar and chocolate. Heat to serving temperature. Serve hot or cold. Yield: 6 servings.

Esta Newman
Bluffs, Illinois

BLUSH PUNCH

1 12-oz. can frozen orange juice
1 3-oz. package lemonade mix
1/4 c. sugar
2 qt. cold water
1 can pineapple-grapefruit juice
1 can cranberry juice
1 pt. strong tea
1 qt. ginger ale
Orange sherbet

Combine all ingredients except ginger ale and sherbet. Chill. Add ginger ale and sherbet just before serving time.

Mabel Oxenford
Glidden, Iowa

BANANA-STRAWBERRY PUNCH

5 bananas
1 box fresh strawberries, washed, capped
1/3 c. sugar
1 qt. chilled extra dry champagne
1 pt. pineapple sherbet (opt.)

Place 4 bananas with strawberries and sugar in blender container. Process to blend. Pour into punch bowl; add champagne. Top with scoops of sherbet. Garnish with several whole or halved strawberries and 1 sliced banana. Yield: 10-12 servings.

PEACHY PUNCH

3 c. peach nectar
1/3 c. honey
2 qt. orange-pineapple juice
1 qt. lemon-lime carbonated beverage

Stir peach nectar into honey gradually; stir in juice. Chill until ready to serve. Add carbonated beverage just before serving.

Brenda Stoeck
Houston, Texas

RECEPTION PUNCH

1 pkg. powdered drink mix
1 can frozen lemonade
1 1/2 c. sugar
1 46-oz. can pineapple juice

Dissolve drink mix in 1 cup hot water; add remaining ingredients with enough water to make 1 gallon punch.

Mrs. Laurena C. Ward
Ashford, Alabama

FROTHY FROZEN PUNCH

2 3-oz. packages flavored gelatin
2 pkg. powdered drink mix
2 c. sugar
1/2 c. lemon juice
1 46-oz. can pineapple juice

Select gelatin and powdered drink mix for desired color. Dissolve gelatin in 2 cups hot water; add drink mix and sugar, stirring to dissolve. Stir in fruit juices. Add 4 1/2 quarts cold water; mix well. Freeze in 1/2-gallon cartons. Remove from freezer about 1 hour before serving; place in punch bowl. Break up with a heavy fork; whip until frothy. Serve at once. Yield: 2 gallons.

Mrs. Annetta Bailey
Agua Dulce, Texas

FRUIT PUNCH FOR A CROWD

4 c. sugar
1/8 tsp. salt
1 qt. strong tea
1 lge. can orange juice
1 1-pt. bottle lemon juice
4 qt. ice water
1 lge. can pineapple juice
1 qt. ginger ale

Combine sugar, salt and 1 quart water in saucepan; heat, stirring well, until sugar dissolves. Boil for 5 minutes. Cool. Add tea, orange juice, lemon juice, ice water and pineapple juice; chill thoroughly. Pour into punch bowl; add ginger ale and ice ring just before serving. Other fruit juices may be used for different color schemes or holidays.

Mrs. Clara Schmalzle
Eldred, New York

MOCK CHAMPAGNE COCKTAIL

1/2 c. sugar
1 1/2 c. water
2 c. cranberry juice
2 c. pineapple juice
1 c. orange juice
1 lge. bottle ginger ale

Boil sugar and water for 3 minutes; cool. Blend in fruit juices. Pour in ginger ale just before serving. Yield: 24 servings.

Mrs. Merle Tevesme
Arcadia, Wisconsin

WINE PARTY PUNCH

2 6-oz. cans frozen Hawaiian punch
2 6-oz. cans frozen orange juice concentrate
2 bottles Sauterne, chilled
2 qt. club soda, chilled
1 pt. whole strawberries
1 c. sliced peaches

Mix frozen juices and Sauterne together in punch bowl until juices are thawed. Add ice ring. Pour in club soda just before serving. Garnish with strawberries and peaches. Yield: Fifty 3-ounce servings.

Mrs. Karin Bargar
Lansing, Michigan

MAKING JELLY WITH CANNED FRUIT JUICES

Never throw away leftover fruit juices. Prepare jelly as with fresh fruit juices, but with less sugar. Follow directions on fruit pectin package; add 1 tablespoon lemon juice and better results will be acquired.

Sister Constance Herbers
Granville, Iowa

APPLE PEELING JELLY

Peelings and cores of 15 to 20 med. tart apples
1 box pectin
9 c. sugar
Red food coloring
Paraffin

Cook peelings and cores in 6 cups water in saucepan for 20 to 30 minutes; strain through a cloth. Add enough water to strained juice to make 7 cups liquid. Add pectin; bring to a rapid boil. Add sugar and food coloring; boil for 1 minute. Pour into sterilized jelly glasses; top with 1/8 inch melted paraffin. Yield: 6 cups.

Mrs. Carolyn Gregory
Latham, Ohio

APPLE-TOMATO JELLY

1 1/4 c. apple juice
1 c. tomato juice
5 c. sugar
1/2 c. lemon juice
1/2 tsp. onion juice
Several dashes of Tabasco sauce
1/4 tsp. ground cloves
1 bottle liquid fruit pectin
Paraffin

Combine apple juice, tomato juice, sugar, lemon juice, onion juice, Tabasco sauce and cloves in large saucepan. Bring to a boil over high heat, stirring constantly. Stir in fruit pectin. Bring to a full rolling boil. Boil for 1 minute, stirring constantly. Remove from heat; skim off foam with metal spoon. Pour into hot sterilized jelly glasses; cover with 1/8 inch hot paraffin. Yield: 6 glasses.

APPLESAUCE-GINGER JAM

4 c. canned applesauce
4 1/2 c. sugar
1/2 c. crystallized ginger, chopped
4 tbsp. lemon juice
1/8 tsp. each cinnamon, ginger
1/2 bottle liquid fruit pectin
Paraffin

Combine applesauce, sugar, crystallized ginger, lemon juice, cinnamon and ginger in large saucepan. Bring to a boil over high heat, stirring constantly. Stir in fruit pectin. Bring to a full rolling boil. Boil for 1 minute, stirring constantly. Remove from heat; skim off foam with metal spoon. Pour into hot sterilized jelly glasses; seal with 1/8 inch hot paraffin. Yield: 11 glasses.

ORANGE MARMALADE

1 lb. apricots, chopped
1 lge. can pineapple
Juice of 2 oranges
Grated rind of 1 orange
4 c. sugar

Cook apricots until tender. Add remaining ingredients. Cook over low heat for 30 to 45 minutes.

Edwina Carmichael
Stevensville, Minnesota

INSTANT RHUBARB JAM

10 c. chopped rhubarb
6 c. sugar
6 c. strawberries
3 pkg. strawberry gelatin

Cover rhubarb with sugar; let stand overnight. Add strawberries; bring to a boil. Remove from heat; add gelatin. Pour into small jars. Store in refrigerator. Yield: 8 pints.

Hermione Crawford
Danbury, Connecticut

RIPE TOMATO MARMALADE

1/2 peck ripe tomatoes, chopped
3 oranges, ground
Juice of 2 lemons
8 c. sugar
1 lb. chopped walnuts

Partially cook tomatoes; pour off most of juice. Add next 3 ingredients. Boil slowly, until thick, stirring frequently. Add walnuts. Pour into small jars; seal.

Carla Wisner
Woodrow, New Hampshire

CRANBERRY-ORANGE RELISH

2 oranges
1 pkg. cranberries
2 c. sugar

Quarter oranges; remove seeds. Grind oranges and cranberries together; stir in sugar. Cover; refrigerate for several hours before serving. Yield: 6-8 servings.

Mrs. Mae Van Petett
Tompkinsville, Kentucky

SWEET CORN RELISH

18 ears sweet corn
2 lge. green peppers
2 sweet red peppers
1 sm. cabbage
4 onions
1 c. chopped celery
1 qt. vinegar
2 c. (firmly packed) brown sugar
2 tbsp. salt
3 tbsp. mustard

Cut corn kernels from cobs. Seed and chop peppers. Chop cabbage and onions. Combine vegetables in large kettle. Add remaining ingredients; mix well. Cook, stirring occasionally for about 30 minutes or until vegetables are tender. Pack into hot sterilized jars; seal. Yield: 5 pints.

Mrs. Wilbur Nye
Green Springs, Ohio

PICCALILLI

2 qt. sliced green tomatoes
1 pt. chopped onions
1 pt. sliced green peppers
1 qt. shredded cabbage
1 pt. thinly sliced carrots
1 pt. chopped celery

2 oz. mustard seed
1 tsp. turmeric
4 tbsp. salt
2 lb. sugar
2 qt. white vinegar

Place all ingredients in large kettle; mix well. Cook slowly for 1 hour, stirring occasionally. Pour into hot sterilized jars; seal at once. Yield: 12 pints.

Mrs. Pauline Moxley
McAllen, Texas

RELISHED CARROTS

1/2 c. apple vinegar
1/2 c. salad oil
3/4 c. sugar
1 can whole baby carrots
1 tbsp. chopped pimento
1/2 c. green pickle relish

Heat vinegar, salad oil and sugar in saucepan; add carrots. Chill overnight. Drain. Add pimento and pickle relish; serve.

Mrs. Billye Freeland
El Paso, Texas

MAKING CHILI SAUCE FROM CATSUP

An easily prepared and economical homemade chili sauce to use for barbecue sauce or on salads may be made by adding 1/2 teaspoon instant minced onion, 1/4 teaspoon chili powder and 1/8 teaspoon pepper to 1 cup catsup.

Evelyn B. Willey
Gatesville, North Carolina

MICROWAVE SAUCES FOR VEGETABLES

1 c. milk
2 tbsp. butter
2 tbsp. flour
Pepper to taste

Microwave milk in glass measure on Medium-High for 2 minutes. Microwave butter in 2-cup glass measure on High for 45 seconds. Blend in flour. Microwave on High for 1 minute. Stir in milk with wire whisk. Add pepper. Microwave on High for 3 minutes or until thickened. Serve over vegetables. Yield: 1 cup.

Cheese Sauce: Use slightly less flour. Stir in shredded cheese until melted. Cheese will thicken sauce as it melts.

Mustard Sauce: Add 1/2 teaspoon dry mustard dissolved in 2 teaspoons water.

Curry Sauce: Add 1/2 to 1 teaspoon curry powder mixed with 2 teaspoons water.

Parsley Sauce: Add 2 tablespoons chopped fresh parsley or 2 teaspoons parsley flakes.

Chive Sauce: Add 2 tablespoons chopped fresh chives or 2 teaspoons dried chives.

Dill Sauce: Add 1 to 2 teaspoons dillweed.

Carol Workman
Portland, Oregon

ALL-SUMMER BARBECUE SAUCE

1 qt. tomato juice
1/2 c. Worcestershire sauce
1 sm. jar mustard
1 1-lb. box brown sugar
1/2 sm. can pepper
2 bottles catsup
2 bottles hickory-flavored barbecue sauce
2 tbsp. garlic salt
1/2 c. salt
1 6-oz. can tomato paste
1 pt. white vinegar
1 1/2 pt. salad oil
1 lge. onion, chopped
1 can beer

Mix all ingredients in large saucepan; bring to a boil. Reduce heat; simmer for 1 hour. Place in sterilized jars; seal. Yield: 5 quarts.

Janet Wommack
Odessa, Texas

Salads & Sandwiches

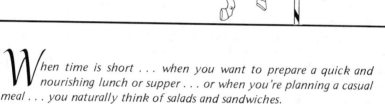

When time is short . . . when you want to prepare a quick and nourishing lunch or supper . . . or when you're planning a casual meal . . . you naturally think of salads and sandwiches.

Sandwiches and salads come in many forms. In fact, just about any kind of food . . . whether meat, vegetable, fruit, egg, or cheese . . . can be transformed into a delicious salad or sandwich.

With all their versatility, salads and sandwiches are still the thrifty homemaker's best friends. Women appreciate the low-cost aspect of these dishes and, in the pages that follow, America's budget-minded homemakers share their favorite low-cost salad and sandwich recipes with you.

Accompanying these taste-tempting recipes are money-saving hints on getting the most for your salad and sandwich dollar. You'll discover how to turn dried cheese into a smooth and delicious cheese spread . . . how to revive limp lettuce . . . and many other cherished secrets.

As you read through these pages, you'll find yourself imagining new ways to turn leftovers into salads and sandwiches that are uniquely yours — creative, imaginative dishes that reflect your skill as a cook . . . and as a thrifty homemaker.

Salads & Sandwiches

GETTING MORE FOR YOUR MONEY

SALADS . . .

are important for your family's well-being — in fact, most home economists recommend that you serve leafy green vegetables at least once a day because they are rich in needed vitamins and iron. And what a boon salads are to your budget! Salad greens are in season nearly all year. And the budget-wise addition of leftover meats, cheese, and eggs to a basic green salad can transform it into a meal in itself.

When you are shopping, visit the produce section after all your other marketing is done. If it is the first time you have visited a store, you'll want to check the cleanliness and temperature of the produce section — salad vegetables spoil if the temperature is too warm. Notice how the produce is handled. Are stock boys cutting off the spoiled parts and returning produce to the counter? Is the fresh produce being placed beneath older stock? If the answer to either of these questions is yes, then don't buy. You will be getting inferior stock with few vitamin and mineral values intact.

Assuming that you have found a good produce section, check to see how the produce is wrapped. Ideally, you should be able to buy salad greens loose — so that you can see the entire vegetable and check it thoroughly. But you're apt to find most vegetables pre-packaged. Some types of packaging — the so-called lattice packages — let you see all around the vegetable. But other kinds, especially those with a cardboard base, don't let you see the bottom of the vegetables. Result: you may get a poor head of lettuce or spoiled celery.

Consider local sources of garden vegetables. Large chain grocery outlets may not have either the freshest or best looking salad greens available. They must purchase from large suppliers, not local farmers who grow small quantities. But some of the locally owned grocery stores in your community, the curb markets, or even highway fruit and vegetable stands may be sources of that carefully tended, farm-fresh produce which is every homemaker's goal. Check your local resources — you may be pleasantly surprised at what is available!

Lettuce is the heart of any salad. It's one of your best buys in the spring and summer months. For economy and variety, try low-cost types of lettuce — romaine, escarole, endive, and bibb. For interesting additions, introduce your family to young spinach leaves, dandelion greens, or other favorite greens from your local gardens.

Whatever your family's preference for salad ingredients, they are probably unanimous in their desire for a great dressing. You'll pay up to a dollar for a small bottle of prepared dressing that isn't half as good as one you prepare at home – at far less cost. A good basic dressing mixes three or four parts olive oil with one part vinegar or lemon juice. You might flavor the vinegar with a touch of tarragon or rosemary. You will find many other economical recipes on the following pages.

To save on the high cost of olive oil, buy your oil in an Italian grocery store if you have one near you – it costs far less and is superior in quality. And you might mix one part olive oil with two parts vegetable oil – the flavor is about the same and the cost is far less.

Spark up your salad dressing with a touch of mustard . . . garlic . . . salt and pepper . . . or your family's favorite herbs and spices. Result: a salad dressing that is uniquely yours, at a cost far below what you would pay for prepared dressings.

SANDWICHES . . .

may be the ever popular two (or more) slices of bread with filling between the slices or the European open-faced sandwich. Both types feature hot or cold fillings, sweet ones, tart ones . . . something sure to please everyone's taste.

Bread is the basis of your sandwich. The best sandwich breads are a day old – this means you can take advantage of a local bakery outlet where they sell day-old bread for as little as 30 cents a loaf! To cut down the cost of your poor boy sandwiches, try slicing French or Italian bread in 6- to 8-inch lengths – the bread costs less than the usual rolls and goes farther!

Butter is a must for successful sandwich making. As a thrifty homemaker, you'll probably want to substitute margarine for butter: it costs about half as much and is far better for your family . . . margarine has fewer fats than does butter. Cream the butter or margarine until it reaches spreading consistency. For unusual flavor treats, try creaming one of your favorite seasonings into the butter. Mustard, horseradish, parsley, chive, curry powder, minced onion, celery salt, even a light hint of garlic . . . will bring a welcome note of flavor to your sandwiches.

Fillings can be prepared from almost anything you have on hand in your kitchen cupboards or refrigerator. Combine that leftover roast beef with a 25-cent can of beef gravy, add your own touch with seasonings, and serve your family hot roast beef sandwiches! For lighter sandwiches, try softening a package of cream cheese and adding some chopped nuts. And don't forget the many delicious salad spreads – the list of possible fillings is limited only by the leftovers you have on hand.

FREEZING BANANAS

Buy bananas when on special. Mash; sprinkle with ascorbic acid powder. Freeze in measured amounts. Bananas are ready to use in any recipe.

Mrs. Larry Clark
Chilocco, Oklahoma

FROZEN BANANA SALAD

1/2 tsp. salt
1 1/2 to 2 tbsp. vinegar
1 1/2 tbsp. flour
1/4 c. sugar
3/4 c. pineapple juice
1 egg
3 bananas, crushed
1 c. diced pineapple
12 maraschino cherries, chopped
1 c. diced pears
1 c. whipped cream
Chopped nuts

Combine salt, vinegar, flour, sugar, pineapple juice and egg in double boiler. Cook, stirring constantly, until thick; cool. Add bananas, pineapple, cherries and pears. Fold in whipped cream. Pour into 2 trays; freeze. Garnish with nuts and additional whipped cream if desired. Yield: 12 servings.

Leona Ferch Smith
Sunnyside, Washington

ALWAYS READY FROZEN FRUIT SALAD

1 3-oz. package cream cheese
2 tbsp. cream
2 tbsp. lemon juice
1/8 tsp. salt
1 c. diced pineapple
1/2 c. quartered marshmallows
1 c. quartered maraschino cherries
1 banana, mashed
2 c. whipped cream
3/4 c. mayonnaise

Combine cream cheese, cream, lemon juice and salt; mix until smooth. Add pineapple, marshmallows, cherries and banana. Combine whipped cream and mayonnaise. Fold into fruit mixture. Pour into ice trays; freeze. Serve on lettuce. Yield: 16 servings.

Rachael A. Dix
Montpelier, Vermont

APPLE-CARROT SALAD

3 med. apples, diced
2 carrots, grated
1/2 c. chopped pecans
3 tbsp. sugar
1/2 c. mayonnaise
1/3 c. raisins

Combine apples, carrots and pecans. Mix in sugar and mayonnaise. Add raisins; blend well. Refrigerate until ready to serve. Yield: 6-8 servings.

Mrs. Mildred Bullard
Wilson, North Carolina

REVIVE LIMP CELERY

Place limp celery in deep pitcher or jar; fill with cold water. Place in refrigerator. Celery will become very crisp.

Martha Hughes
Jefferson, Oregon

CITRUS SALAD WITH CRANBERRY DRESSING

1 c. jellied cranberry sauce
1 c. mayonnaise
2 tbsp. lime or lemon juice
1 c. whipped cream (opt.)
Lettuce cups
1 c. orange sections

1 c. grapefruit sections
2 c. melon balls

Blend cranberry sauce and mayonnaise together with electric mixer. Add lime juice; fold in whipped cream. Place lettuce cups in 6 individual serving dishes. Arrange fruits in lettuce cups. Serve with dressing.

Mrs. Thelma Hause
Claremont, New Hampshire

STRAWBERRY SALAD

2 pkg. strawberry gelatin
1 c. hot water
1 c. cold water
2 10-oz. packages frozen strawberries
1 env. dessert topping mix
2 tbsp. sugar
1 3-oz. package soft cream cheese

Dissolve gelatin in hot water; stir in cold water. Add 2 ice cubes; stir until ice cubes are melted. Chill until thickened. Thaw strawberries; add to gelatin mixture. Pour half of the mixture in oblong baking dish. Chill until firm. Chill remaining half of mixture until partially set. Prepare dessert topping mix according to package directions; combine with sugar and cream cheese. Beat until smooth. Spread dessert topping mixture over frozen layer; top with remaining gelatin. Chill for several hours. Yield: 8 servings.

Mrs. Fayma Drummond
Petersburg, Texas

CABBAGE PATCH COLESLAW

2 c. shredded cabbage
1/2 c. chopped parsley
1/2 c. sliced green onions
2 to 3 tbsp. sugar
3 tbsp. vinegar
2 tbsp. salad oil
1 tsp. salt
Green pepper rings
Onion rings

Combine cabbage, parsley and green onions; mix. Combine remaining ingredients except green pepper and onion rings; stir to dissolve sugar. Pour over cabbage mixture; toss. Place green pepper and onion rings on top. Yield: 6 servings.

Collen Lenz
Jordan, Minnesota

GREEN BEAN SALAD

1 onion
1 lge. green pepper
1 can English peas
1 can whole green beans
1 c. diced celery
3/4 c. cider vinegar
1/4 c. garlic wine vinegar
1/2 c. water
1 tbsp. sugar
1/4 c. salad oil
Salt and pepper to taste

Slice onion and green pepper into thin rings. Drain peas and beans. Combine onion, green pepper, peas, beans and celery in large bowl. Combine remaining ingredients; mix well. Pour over vegetables. Cover; refrigerate for 24 hours. Stir well before serving. Yield: 6-8 servings.

Thelma Maxey
Larenzo, Texas

TURNING DRIED CHEESE INTO SPREAD

Stale cheese turns into a delicious spread when processed through the meat grinder with several chunks of onions.

Mrs. D. J. Dear
Stringer, Mississippi

MARINATED GREEN BEAN SALAD

2 pkg. frozen French-style green beans
3 tbsp. cider vinegar
1 1/2 tbsp. salad oil
1 tsp. salt
Dash of pepper
1/2 tsp. chopped parsley

Cook beans according to package directions; drain. Turn into shallow serving dish; refrigerate for 1 hour or until well chilled. Combine remaining ingredients in jar with tight-fitting lid; shake vigorously. Pour over beans; toss gently until well coated. Refrigerate until ready to serve; toss lightly.

Beverly Walsh
Ord, Nebraska

PRACTICAL USES FOR LEFTOVER ROAST BEEF

Leftover roast may be sliced and used in sandwiches or ground and made into spread by mixing with mayonnaise and relish. Chopped roast may be made into a delightful hash, reheated in gravy and served on toast or buns.

Grace Smith
Dalton, Georgia

MIXED VEGETABLE SALAD

1 lb. fresh peas, shelled, cooked
1 lb. fresh lima beans, shelled, cooked
1 c. sliced fresh carrots, cooked
1/3 c. salad oil
3 tbsp. fresh lemon juice
2 tsp. salt
1/8 tsp. pepper
1 clove of garlic, minced
8 c. torn salad greens
1 med. tomato, cut into 8 wedges
1 cucumber, scored, sliced

Drain and chill cooked vegetables. Combine oil, lemon juice, salt, pepper and garlic in jar with tight-fitting lid; shake well. Let stand for 30 minutes. Remove garlic. Marinate cooked vegetables in dressing for 1 hour or longer. Place salad greens in bowl. Arrange tomato, cucumber and marinated vegetables on greens. Yield: 8 servings.

Claudia Horstman
Winslow, Arizona

MICROWAVE HOT BEAN SALAD

6 slices bacon
Vinegar
1 tbsp. cornstarch
1/4 c. sugar
1 16-oz. can wax beans, drained
1 16-oz. can green beans, drained
1 16-oz. can kidney beans, drained
1 onion, sliced into rings

Microwave bacon in glass dish on High for 5 minutes or until crisp. Drain, reserving drippings. Add enough vinegar to drippings to measure 1/2 cup. Blend with cornstarch and sugar in 2-quart glass dish. Microwave on High for 3 minutes or until thickened, stirring twice. Stir in beans and onion. Crumble bacon over top. Microwave on High for 4 to 5 minutes or until heated through.

Joyce Horvath
Wellington, Ohio

BEAN AND BACON SALAD

Cider vinegar
1/4 c. water
1/4 c. sugar
1 pkg. frozen green beans, cooked, drained
1 c. cooked cauliflowerets, drained
1 tbsp. chopped pimento
4 green onions, sliced
1/2 c. diced celery
8 slices crisp-fried bacon, crumbled
1 tbsp. brown sugar
2 tbsp. bacon drippings
1/2 tsp. salt

Add 1/4 cup vinegar, water and sugar to beans. Chill for 2 to 3 hours; drain. Combine beans with remaining vegetables and bacon. Heat remaining ingredients with 2 tablespoons vinegar until sugar dissolves. Pour over vegetables; toss to mix. Serve in lettuce cups.

Carolyn Ewan
Arlington Heights, Illinois

POTATO SALAD WITH BACON

4 slices bacon, diced, cooked
2 tbsp. sugar
1 tsp. salt
1/4 tsp. seasoned pepper
1 tsp. prepared mustard
1/2 tsp. celery seed
1/3 c. vinegar
1 lge. onion, chopped
6 lge. potatoes, cooked, diced

Combine bacon and a small amount of bacon dripping with remaining ingredients except potatoes in pressure cooker. Add potatoes; mix well. Cook for 5 minutes following manufacturer's directions. Reduce pressure immediately. Serve hot or cold. Yield: 6 servings.

Mrs. Aleen Hartman
Manderson, Wyoming

AMERICAN NICOISE SALAD

1 sm. red onion
1 sm. head lettuce
2 7-oz. cans tuna
1 c. sliced cooked potatoes
1 c. cooked green beans
3 hard-cooked eggs, quartered
3 sm. tomatoes, quartered
12 pitted ripe olives
3/4 tsp. salt
Dash of paprika
1/2 tsp. monosodium glutamate
1/3 c. lemon juice or vinegar
2/3 c. salad oil

Slice onion thin; separate into rings. Shred lettuce. Drain tuna and separate into large chunks. Place lettuce in large shallow bowl. Mound tuna in center of bowl; surround with ring of potatoes and beans. Alternate egg and tomato quarters around beans. Garnish with onion and olives. Cover tightly with plastic wrap; refrigerate until chilled. Combine salt, paprika, monosodium glutamate and lemon juice; stir with fork until dry ingredients are dissolved. Add oil; beat with fork until blended. Pour dressing over salad just before serving.

Mrs. Irene Wells
Ulysses, Kansas

CHEF'S SALAD

8 c. chopped mixed salad greens
1 c. diced celery
1 c. cooked ham strips
2 hard-cooked eggs, chopped
2 tbsp. chopped parsley
4 tomatoes, cut in wedges
1 c. garlic or French dressing

Chill all ingredients. Combine all ingredients except dressing; toss. Add dressing; toss again. Yield: 12 servings.

Myrtle Stevens
Gracemont, Oklahoma

TOMATO AND PEPPER SURPRISE SALAD

2 lge. tomatoes, diced
1 lge. green pepper, diced
1 med. onion, diced
1/4 lb. saltine crackers, crumbled
Salt and pepper to taste
2 tbsp. (heaping) mayonnaise

Combine all ingredients; toss lightly. Serve chilled.

Anne G. Rollins
Coward, South Carolina

HINT FOR KEEPING VEGETABLES AND FRUIT FRESH LONGER

Line refrigerator food crisper with 2 layers of paper towels. Towels will absorb the moisture, keeping vegetables and fruits crisper and tastier longer.

Mrs. Jean Bass
Yonkers, New York

SPINACH SALAD

1 c. salad oil
1/2 c. dark vinegar
3/4 c. sugar
2 tsp. salt
1/3 c. catsup
2 bags spinach, torn
2 c. water chestnuts, diced
1 c. bean sprouts, drained
1 Bermuda onion, sliced
4 hard-cooked eggs, chopped
1/2 lb. crisp-cooked bacon, crumbled

Combine oil, vinegar, sugar, salt and catsup; mix well. Combine remaining ingredients; toss with dressing. Yield: 12 servings.

Mrs. Helen Orlyk
Grand Rapids, Michigan

WESTERN TOSSED SALAD

2 cloves of garlic, mashed
2 tsp. salt
1/4 c. lemon juice
1/2 tsp. sugar
1/2 tsp. pepper
1/4 tsp. celery seed
1 tsp. paprika
1 1/2 tsp. dry mustard
10 tbsp. salad oil
2 med. heads lettuce
2 bunches watercress
1 clove of garlic, peeled, cut in half
1 1/2 c. caulifllowerets, chilled
1 ripe avocado, chopped
2 tomatoes, peeled, sliced, chilled
Shredded carrot (opt.)
Shredded cheese (opt.)
Hard-boiled eggs, chopped (opt.)
1 c. toasted blanched almonds, sliced

Combine first 8 ingredients in jar; mix well. Add oil. Cover; shake well. Chill. Tear greens into pieces; chill. Rub salad bowl with cut garlic. Place salad greens, fresh vegetables and remaining ingredients in salad bowl. Add dressing; toss well.

Sister Mary Benedict Beehler, O.S.B.
Crookston, Minnesota

FROZEN FRESH TOMATOES

Purchase fresh ripe tomatoes in summer when plentiful, cheap and of good quality. Cut into wedges or slices; arrange on baking sheets. Freeze. Transfer to plastic bags; tie bags securely with plastic wire fasteners. Store in freezer. Use for salads and casseroles.

Mrs. Catherine Brady
East Orange, New Jersey

DEVILED EGG MOLD

1 env. unflavored gelatin
1/2 c. water
1 tsp. salt
1 to 2 tbsp. lemon juice or vinegar
1/4 tsp. Worcestershire sauce
Cayenne pepper to taste (opt.)
3/4 c. mayonnaise or salad dressing
1 1/2 tsp. grated onion
1/4 to 1/2 c. minced green pepper
1/4 c. chopped pimento
4 hard-cooked eggs, chopped
1/2 c. minced celery

Soften gelatin in cold water; place over hot water to melt. Remove from heat; add salt, lemon juice, Worcestershire sauce and cayenne pepper. Cool. Stir in mayonnaise. Fold in remaining ingredients. Turn into a 3-cup mold or individual molds. Chill until firm.

Sister Mary Louise
Clarksburg, West Virginia

EASY-TO-PEEL FRESH BOILED EGGS

Add 1 tablespoon salt to cold water before boiling eggs.

Mrs. Katherine Arnold
Hume, Missouri

MOLDED EGG SALAD

8 hard-cooked eggs, coarsely chopped
1 c. minced celery
1/4 c. salad dressing
1 tsp. Worcestershire sauce
1 tbsp. lemon juice
1 tsp. scraped onion
Salt and pepper to taste
6 thick tomato slices
Salad greens
Paprika

Combine eggs, celery, dressing, Worcestershire sauce, lemon juice, onion, salt and pepper; mix well. Press into molds; chill. Unmold on tomato slices placed on bed of salad greens. Sprinkle with paprika. Garnish with celery curls and additional seasoning if desired. Yield: 6 servings.

Zelda Leigh Powell
Mandeville, Louisiana

MAIN DISH HAM SALAD

1 can chopped ham, diced
2 hard-cooked eggs, chopped
3 tbsp. chopped sweet pickle
3 tbsp. chopped celery
1 sm. apple, chopped
Salad dressing

Combine all ingredients except salad dressing; mix, adding enough salad dressing to moisten. Chill. Serve on lettuce leaf with hot rolls.

Mrs. Margaret D. Randall
Tallulah, Louisiana

HEARTY MACARONI SALAD

1/2 c. macaroni
1/4 lb. luncheon meat, cubed
1/2 c. canned green peas, chilled
1/2 c. chopped celery
1/4 lb. Cheddar cheese, cubed
1 tbsp. chopped onion
1 tbsp. minced parsley
1/4 c. chopped green pepper
Salt and pepper to taste
1/3 c. salad dressing
1 hard-cooked egg, sliced

Cook macaroni according to package directions; drain. Combine all ingredients except egg; toss. Chill. Garnish with egg slices. Yield: 6 servings.

Mrs. Stewart Knight
Hale Center, Texas

MACARONI SUPPER SALAD

3 c. drained cooked macaroni
3/4 c. chopped cooked ham
3/4 c. chopped cooked chicken
1/4 c. diced celery
1/4 c. minced onion
1/4 c. chopped green pepper
1 pimento, chopped
1/2 c. mayonnaise
Salt and pepper to taste
2 hard-cooked eggs, chopped

Combine all ingredients except eggs; mix well. Garnish with eggs. Yield: 6-8 servings.

Judy Lennon
Achille, Oklahoma

MENDING COOKING EGGS THAT CRACK

If an egg cracks while being cooked in shell, add small amount of vinegar to cooking water to prevent egg white from seeping through shell.

Mrs. John Leischner
DeLand, Illinois

PRESSED CHICKEN SALAD LOAF

1 stewing hen
2 1/2 tsp. salt
3 or 4 peppercorns
2 c. chopped celery
1 c. chopped pecans
6 hard-cooked eggs, chopped
2 env. unflavored gelatin
1/3 c. sugar
1/2 c. lemon juice

Place chicken in large pan with just enough boiling water to cover; add 2 teaspoons salt and peppercorns. Cover; simmer for 3 hours or until tender. Remove chicken from broth; reserve 2 cups broth. Cool chicken. Remove meat from bones; chop. Combine chopped chicken, celery, pecans and eggs; mix well. Press lightly into 2 loaf pans. Soften gelatin in 1 cup cold water. Heat reserved broth to boiling point; add gelatin, stirring to dissolve. Stir in sugar, lemon juice and remaining salt; cool slightly. Pour over chicken mixtures. Chill until firm. Unmold onto lettuce. Serve with mayonnaise. Yield: 12 servings.

Dena L. Eidson
Corpus Christi, Texas

QUICK AND EASY LUNCHES

Prepare sandwiches from leftover meats. Freeze. Sandwiches are ready as needed for packed lunches and will be thawed by lunch time.

Mrs. John Sennett
Wahoo, Nebraska

WALDORF CHICKEN SALAD

2 c. chopped cooked chicken
1/2 c. diced celery
1/2 c. chopped cucumber pickle
1/2 apple, diced
4 hard-cooked eggs, chopped
2 tbsp. chicken broth
1/4 c. mayonnaise
1 tbsp. pickle juice
Lettuce

Combine all ingredients except lettuce; mix lightly. Arrange on lettuce leaves; garnish with pimento strips if desired.

Mrs. Christine W. Moore
Lena, Mississippi

CREAMY BLUE CHEESE DRESSING

1 env. garlic salad dressing mix
1/2 c. sour cream
1/4 c. chopped sm. green onions
1/2 c. crumbled blue cheese

Prepare garlic salad dressing mix according to package directions. Add sour cream, onions and blue cheese gradually; mix well.

Mrs. Mary Westfoll
Colusa, California

CELERY SEED DRESSING WITH LEMON

1/2 c. sugar
1 tsp. celery seed
1 tsp. salt
1 tsp. dry mustard
1 tsp. paprika
1/3 c. lemon juice
3/4 c. salad oil

Combine all ingredients except oil. Add oil gradually, beating with electric mixer until thick. Yield: 1 1/2 cups.

Elaine M. Krick
Alexandria, Minnesota

WASHING LEAFY VEGETABLES

Add a small amount of vinegar to water in which leafy vegetables are being washed. Any insects, especially on lettuce and spinach, will leave the leaf with vinegar and vigor!

Karenann Manley
Granby, Colorado

EASY THOUSAND ISLAND DRESSING

Dash of salt
1/3 c. drained pickle relish
1/2 c. mayonnaise
1/2 c. chili sauce
2 hard-cooked eggs, coarsely chopped

Combine all ingredients except eggs; blend well. Add eggs. Chill.

Mrs. George Sanders
Hoffman, Minnesota

FAVORITE THOUSAND ISLAND DRESSING

2 eggs
1/2 tsp. mustard
1/4 tsp. salt
3 tbsp. sugar
2 tbsp. vinegar
Dash of paprika
Dash of red pepper
2 c. salad oil
1 1/2 c. catsup
1 sm. can pimentos, drained, finely chopped
1 sm. onion, finely grated
1/2 c. drained sweet pickle relish

Beat eggs until thick; stir in mustard, salt, sugar, vinegar, paprika and red pepper. Add salad oil gradually, beating constantly until dressing is thick. Add catsup gradually; stir in pimentos, onion and pickle relish. Store in covered jar in refrigerator for several hours before using. Yield: 1 quart.

Julie Williams
Salem, Oregon

PIZZA BURGERS

3/4 lb. ground beef
1/3 c. grated Parmesan cheese
1/4 c. onion flakes
1 tsp. salt
1 6-oz. can tomato paste
1/4 c. sliced ripe olives
4 English muffins, split
Sharp grated cheese

Combine first 6 ingredients in skillet; heat through. Spread beef mixture on muffins. Broil for 10 to 12 minutes, 5 inches from source of heat. Top with grated cheese; return to broiler until cheese is melted. Yield: 8 servings.

Mrs. Eleanor Roberts
Benton, Illinois

CORNED BEEF CHEESEBURGER

1 12-oz. can corned beef, chopped
3 tbsp. finely chopped onion
1 tbsp. prepared mustard
3 tbsp. mayonnaise
1 1/2 tsp. horseradish
3 tbsp. butter or margarine
9 hamburger buns, split
9 slices American cheese
Butter

Combine all ingredients except buns, cheese and butter. Mix well. Spread buns with butter. Spoon corned beef mixture on bottom halves of buns; top with slices of cheese. Toast under broiler until cheese melts. Toast bun tops; place over cheese slices. Serve immediately. Yield: 9 servings.

Mrs. William H. Buxton
Cowden, Illinois

PEPPER KRAUT ROUND DOGS

1/2 c. diced green pepper
1/4 c. chopped onion
2 tbsp. butter or margarine
3 1/2 c. sauerkraut, drained
1 tsp. celery seed
Dash of pepper
8 frankfurters
4 hard poppy seed rolls, split
Mayonnaise
8 tomato slices

Saute green pepper and onion in butter until crisp-tender. Stir in sauerkraut, celery seed and pepper. Cover; cook for 8 to 10 minutes or until heated through. Cut 10 deep slits in each frankfurter without cutting all the way through. Broil 5 to 7 inches from source of heat or cook on outdoor grill for 3 to 4 minutes. Turn and broil 3 minutes longer. Spread roll halves with mayonnaise; top each with tomato slice, sauerkraut mixture and round dog.

SWISS HAM SANDWICH

1/3 c. prepared mustard
1/3 c. mayonnaise
2 tbsp. finely chopped onion
1/2 tsp. salt
Dash of pepper
8 buns
8 slices ham
8 slices Swiss cheese

Combine mustard, mayonnaise, onion, salt and pepper. Spread buns with mustard mixture. Place 1 slice of ham and cheese in each bun. Wrap buns in foil; place on baking sheet. Bake at 350 degrees for 20 minutes.

Mrs. Robert Tuttle
DePue, Illinois

FREEZING SANDWICHES FOR LUNCHES

Frozen mayonnaise has a tendency to separate. Use salad dressing, butter or margarine on sandwiches to be frozen. Sandwiches may be prepared for 1 week's lunches and placed in the freezer. Sandwiches will thaw by lunchtime.

Mrs. Betty Johnson
Milwaukee, Wisconsin

BUYING BREAD FOR SANDWICHES

Day-old bread is excellent for making sandwiches and can bring about a saving if bought in quantity at a bakery outlet and placed in the freezer.

Mrs. Irene Kathy Lee
El Dorado, Arkansas

CHICKENBURGERS

2 c. minced cooked chicken
1/4 c. chopped almonds
1/2 tsp. grated onion
1/4 c. dry bread crumbs
2 tsp. chopped parsley
1 tsp. lemon juice
1/4 c. milk
Salt and pepper to taste
2 to 4 tbsp. melted butter
8 hamburger bun halves, toasted

Mix all ingredients together except butter and buns. Shape into 8 patties. Place on broiler tray; brush with melted butter. Broil on both sides until browned. Serve on toasted buns. Yield: 8 servings.

Mrs. Raymond Brown
Pensacola, Florida

CHICKEN ON A BUN

2 7-oz. cans boned chicken
1/4 c. chopped stuffed olives
3/4 c. diced celery
3/4 c. chopped sweet pickles
2 tbsp. chopped onion
1/2 c. mayonnaise
8 hamburger buns
Butter
16 slices American cheese

Combine chicken, olives, celery, pickles and onion; add mayonnaise. Slice buns into halves; spread with butter. Spread chicken mixture on buns; top with 1 slice cheese. Place buns on cookie sheet. Bake at 350 degrees for 10 to 15 minutes or until cheese is melted. Yield: 16 sandwiches.

Mrs. Vernon Greene
Chicago, Illinois

CLUB SANDWICHES

8 slices toast
Salad dressing
8 slices cooked turkey
4 lge. slices tomato
16 slices bacon, fried
8 leaves lettuce

Spread toast with salad dressing. Place 2 slices turkey, 1 slice tomato, 4 slices bacon and 2 lettuce leaves on each of 4 slices toast. Cover with remaining toast. Cut diagonally into fourths. Yield: 4 servings.

Mrs. Fred Owens
Lexington, Kentucky

POOR RICHARD'S RAREBIT SANDWICH

2 tbsp. butter
2 tbsp. flour
1 c. milk
2 c. shredded American cheese
1/2 tsp. mustard
1 tsp. Worcestershire sauce
Salt to taste
6 slices crisp toast
Sliced cooked chicken
Paprika

Melt butter in saucepan over low heat; blend in flour. Add milk, stirring constantly. Cook, stirring, until sauce is smooth and thickened. Add cheese, mustard, Worcestershire sauce and salt. Stir over low heat only until cheese is melted. Arrange toast in individual custard cups or shallow baking pan; top with slices of chicken. Cover with cheese sauce; sprinkle lightly with paprika. Heat under broiler until cheese sauce is lightly browned.

Mrs. Susan Haigler
Fort Deposit, Alabama

BAY LEAF
Salt

Soups & Stews

Bubbling pots of appetite-arousing liquid . . . bright vegetables in a shimmering broth . . . great chunks of meat cooked to perfection . . . welcome to the wonderful world of soups and stews.

It is a wonderful world, not only of flavor and nutritional values, but of economy as well. For generations thrifty homemakers have taken scraps of meat, bone, and vegetables and slowly simmered them into rich soups . . . have simmered inexpensive cuts of meats and older, less costly vegetables for hours to create mouth-watering stews.

Now, in one richly varied section, America's thrifty homemakers share with you their secrets for making family-pleasing soups and stews. Every hint in these pages . . . every recipe . . . has been developed by a woman like you, in her own kitchen. These are the things conscientious homemakers depend upon to make their food dollars stretch . . . and bring them warm words of praise from family and friends alike. Among the recipes you'll find vegetable soup . . . gumbo . . . hearty beef stews.

The next time you are confronted with a hungry family . . . and need for a low-cost meal . . . turn to this section. You'll be able to prepare a taste-tempting, homemade soup or stew at only pennies per serving!

Soups & Stews

GETTING MORE FOR YOUR MONEY

Soups and stews are among the most economical dishes you can serve to your family – and among the most nutritious. Both combine meats and vegetables in a liquid which is then simmered over low heat for hours. This liquid draws many of the nutrients from the meat and vegetables and is a marvelous source of vitamins and minerals.

Soup is prepared from a base of stock. Stock is liquid in which meat scraps, bones, and vegetables have been cooked until they are flavorless. All of their flavor and nutritional values have become concentrated in the stock.

There are two kinds of stock: brown, made from beef and ham scraps which have been browned or roasted; and white, made from chicken or veal scraps. Stock also contains vegetables – most frequently carrots, celery, and onions – for added flavor.

Stock made with bones and no meat scraps will take on an unpleasant flavor. The best stocks have plenty of raw and cooked meat scraps. Chicken wings, backs, necks, and gizzards are low in cost but make a richly flavored stock of incomparable quality. And when you next ask the butcher to bone or trim any piece of meat for you, be sure to ask for the scraps – they're perfect for stock.

Stock is most often prepared in the family stockpot, a large iron pot which sits simmering on the back of the stove. Into this pot go meat scraps, bones, bits of fat (browned), potato peelings, carrot tops . . . in short, everything that can be used to flavor the liquid.

You may wish to add additional flavorings in the form of herbs. Use a very light touch. The stock will be boiled down as it cooks, concentrating the flavors. The seasonings you use will also be concentrated – if you have used a heavy touch, the effect may be overwhelming.

Stock is used to make three basic kinds of soups. First, stock with the fat skimmed off is known as *bouillon* or broth. Clarified stock is called *consomme.*

Stock is also the base of such light, thin soups as *bisque* or vegetable cream soup. Incidentally, this latter soup is a wonderful way to use up those bits and pieces of leftover vegetables you've been holding on to.

Thin, light soups make delicious first courses. Be sure to match your soup to your main course. Fruit soup is especially nice with chicken or veal while bouillon or consomme is a delightful beginning to a hearty beef dinner. Add a sandwich and a salad to one of these light soups, and you'll have a perfect luncheon or supper. In summertime, substitute chilled or jellied soups for hot ones — they'll cool off your family and guests wonderfully!

And finally, there are the *heavy, thick soups* — many of which are a meal in themselves! These rich soups include the gumbos, the meat and vegetable soups, and the chowders.

Stews — like soups — are made by simmering meats and vegetables in a liquid over low heat. And like soups, stews are rich in much-needed vitamins and minerals. They are also a boon for thrifty homemakers — a pound of stewing beef, usually selling for around a dollar — will make enough stew to serve four people.

Stews also make economical use of older, lower-priced vegetables. Older carrots, potatoes, onions, and celery are all excellent buys at your produce counter . . . and are just what you need for a flavorful stew.

The older, tougher cuts of meats and vegetables are best for stews because of the cooking method used. Stewing is done with moist heat — heat which softens tough connective tissues and makes them tender. Moist heat would take all the flavor out of young, tender vegetables and meat. But it brings out the full, rich flavor of more sinewy meats and older vegetables. In fact, the long, slow cooking process brings out the very best in your every ingredient.

Ready-cut stew meat is available from your grocery store. However, if you're planning beef stew, you might want to buy a large chuck roast to save money. A five-pound chuck roast on sale will usually cost about $1.75 a pound and will yield one pound of stewing meat, a one-and-one-half pound Swiss steak, and a good-sized pot roast. If the difference between the price of the chuck roast and the pre-cut stewing meat is as much as 25 cents, then it may be worth your while to prepare your own stewing beef. Similar savings can be found when veal and lamb are on special. In fact, if you've been a particularly good customer, your butcher may cut these roasts up for you at no extra charge!

The meat for stews is usually cut into one-inch cubes and thoroughly browned. The browning seals in the juices and also brings a rich, dark color to the stewing liquid. After browning, add the liquid and the seasonings you desire. But use a light hand — the stewing liquid will become concentrated as the cooking process continues, and seasoning flavors will also concentrate.

Vegetables for stew are usually added 45 minutes to an hour before cooking time is up. The most commonly used stew vegetables are carrots, onions, and potatoes, but many people also use turnips and cabbage. You may also want to prepare dumplings to cook during the last 20 minutes of stewing time.

DILLED SPLIT PEA SOUP

3 strips bacon
1 tsp. salt
1 c. split peas, well rinsed
1/4 c. finely chopped onion
1 tall can evaporated milk
1/2 tsp. dillweed
Dash of cayenne pepper

Fry bacon until crisp. Drain on absorbent paper. Reserve 2 tablespoons bacon drippings. Combine 3 cups water, salt and peas in medium saucepan; bring to a boil. Boil for 2 minutes. Remove from heat; let stand for 1 hour. Add reserved bacon drippings and onion to peas. Cover saucepan; bring to a boil. Boil slowly for about 40 minutes or until peas are tender. Add milk, dillweed and cayenne pepper. Heat to serving temperature, do not boil. Crumble bacon on top.

MICROWAVE POTATO AND CORN CHOWDER

4 slices bacon
1 onion, chopped
2 medium potatoes, peeled, chopped
1 17-oz. can corn, drained
1 can cream of celery soup
1 1/4 c. milk
1/2 tsp. garlic salt
1/8 tsp. pepper

Place bacon in 2-quart glass dish; cover with paper towel. Microwave on High for 4 minutes or until crisp. Remove bacon; drain all but 2 teaspoons drippings. Add onion, potatoes and 1/4 cup water to drippings. Microwave, covered, for 4 to 5 minutes or until potatoes are almost tender, stirring once. Add corn, soup, milk and seasonings; mix well. Microwave, covered, for 9 minutes or until heated through, stirring once. Ladle into soup bowls. Crumble bacon over top.

Bonnie Platt
Tempe, Arizona

EASY VEGETABLE SOUP

1 lb. ground beef
2 tbsp. lard or drippings
1 tsp. salt
1 bay leaf
1 lge. onion, sliced
1/2 c. chopped celery
1 can consomme
1 1/2 c. water
1 1-lb. 13-oz. can tomatoes
1 10-oz. package frozen mixed vegetables

Brown beef in lard in large kettle. Add remaining ingredients except mixed vegetables. Cover tightly; simmer for 2 hours. Add vegetables; bring to a boil. Reduce heat; simmer for 30 minutes longer or until vgetables are done. Remove bay leaf before serving.

Shirley H. Travis
Tucker, Georgia

DANISH SOUP

6 med. carrots, diced
4 med. potatoes, diced
1 med. onion, diced
2 stalks celery, diced
1 tsp. salt
1/2 lb. ground beef
1/4 tsp. sage
1/4 tsp. pepper
1 egg, beaten

1/2 slice bread, crumbled
1 tbsp. cream
1 1/2 tbsp. flour
1 c. beef bouillon
2 tbsp. minced parsley

Combine carrots, potatoes, onion and celery in pressure cooker; add 1/2 teaspoon salt and 1/2 cup water. Cook for 3 minutes at 15 pounds pressure. Let pressure reduce normally. Combine beef, remaining salt, sage, pepper, egg, bread, cream and flour. Mix well; shape into small balls. Pour bouillon into saucepan; add 1 1/2 cups water. Bring to a boil. Drop meatballs into hot bouillon mixture; cook for about 8 minutes. Add cooked vegetables and parsley; simmer until heated through. Yield: 6 servings.

Mitzi Brandt
Fairborn, Ohio

FREEZING LEFTOVER SOUP FOR EASY USE

Freeze leftover soups in ice cube tray. Remove from tray; package in freezer bag. Store in freezer. Thaw soup cubes as needed in saucepan over low heat.

LaJune Garner
Kansas City, Missouri

GROUND BEEF SOUP

1 med. onion, diced
3 tbsp. cooking oil
1 lb. ground beef
1 tsp. salt
1/2 tsp. pepper
Celery salt to taste
Onion salt to taste
Garlic salt to taste
1 tbsp. parsley flakes
2 tbsp. Worcestershire sauce
1/2 c. rice
2 potatoes, diced
3 carrots, diced
2 stalks celery, chopped
1 No. 303 can tomatoes
1 c. cooked elbow spaghetti
1 can tomato sauce

Saute onion in oil in large kettle. Add beef, seasonings, parsley flakes and Worcestershire sauce; stir over medium heat until beef is browned. Add rice, potatoes, carrots, celery and about 2 quarts water; bring to a boil. Stir well; reduce heat. Simmer until rice and vegetables are tender. Add tomatoes, spaghetti and tomato sauce; mix well. Add water if needed. Return to a boil. Reduce heat; simmer until heated through.

Mrs. Mary A. Campbell
Fort Necessity, Louisiana

WHITE BEAN SOUP

2 c. navy beans
1 meaty ham bone
1/2 c. mashed potatoes
3 onions, finely chopped
1 stalk celery, chopped
1 clove of garlic, minced
1/4 c. minced parsley

Soak beans overnight in 3 quarts water. Add ham bone; bring to a boil. Reduce heat; simmer for 1 hour. Add potatoes, onions, celery, garlic and parsley; mix well. Simmer for 1 hour. Remove ham bone; cut ham from bone. Return ham to soup; heat through.

Mrs. Lillian Herman
Bay City, Texas

FREEZING SOUP IN MILK CARTONS

Rinse empty milk cartons well. Pour in cooled soup. Freeze. Hold carton under warm water until soup thaws enough around edges to slip from carton.

Mrs. Mary McKinney
Calumet City, Illinois

MISER'S WAY FOR HOMEMADE SOUP INGREDIENTS

Save liquid from meats and canned vegetables. Pour into freezer containers; freeze. Small bits of leftover foods may be added to containers and frozen. Thaw frozen mixture; add meat, vegetables or noodles to make a nutritious flavorful soup or stew.

Mrs. Anita Holmes
Copperas Cove, Texas

ECONOMICAL VEGETABLE SOUP

1 lge. potato, diced
1 carrot, diced
1 onion, diced
2 stalks celery, diced
1 tsp. salt
1 tbsp. butter or margarine
1 tsp. monosodium glutamate
Pepper to taste
1/8 tsp. garlic salt
1 1/2 c. skim milk

Combine all ingredients except milk in saucepan; stir in 2 cups water. Cook, tightly covered, over medium heat for 20 minutes; mash. Stir in milk; bring to boiling point. Serve immediately. Yield: 4-6 servings.

Mrs. Winifred McCoy
Follansbee, West Virginia

CREOLE CHICKEN GUMBO

Salt and pepper to taste
Flour
1 chicken, disjointed
Bacon drippings
1 lge. onion, chopped
3 green onions, finely chopped
4 cloves of garlic
1/2 c. chopped celery
1 hot green pepper
1 green pepper, chopped
2 c. chopped okra
1/4 c. chopped parsley
1/2 tsp. thyme
2 bay leaves
2 qt. water

Combine salt, pepper and about 1/2 cup flour; dredge chicken in seasoned flour. Brown chicken well in small amount of bacon drippings in large heavy saucepan. Remove chicken from pan. Add about 6 tablespoons bacon drippings to pan; blend in 3 tablespoons flour. Cook over low heat, stirring constantly, until flour is deep rich brown. Add onions, garlic, celery and peppers; simmer for 10 minutes. Cook okra in a small amount of bacon drippings until dry; add to onion mixture. Stir in parsley, thyme, bay leaves and water; mix well. Return chicken to pan; simmer until chicken is tender.

Mrs. Norine R. Edwards
Kilbourne, Louisiana

SAVING BONES FOR BEEF-VEGETABLE SOUP

Remove bones from steaks and roasts before cooking. Wrap bones for freezing. Save until enough bones have accumulated to make large kettle of soup. Freeze soup in meal-sized containers. Thaw soup. Heat and serve.

Mary Baughn
Victoria, British Columbia, Canada

GOLDEN NUGGET BUDGET SOUP

3 med. potatoes, diced
2 carrots, diced
1 med. onion, diced
1 c. whole kernel corn
2 tbsp. margarine
Salt and pepper to taste
1 can cream of chicken soup
2 c. milk

Combine vegetables and margarine in soup kettle; add water to cover. Bring to a boil. Reduce heat; simmer until vegetables are tender. Stir in seasonings, soup and milk; heat through gently. Yield: 4 servings.

Lorna Hinson
Hickory Grove, South Carolina

CLAM CHOWDER

6 to 8 lge. clams
2 strips bacon
2 onions, chopped
2 qt. water
1 lge. can stewed tomatoes
2 carrots, diced
2 stalks celery, chopped
1/2 tsp. thyme
1/2 tsp. pepper
2 potatoes, diced

Shuck clams, reserving liquid. Fry bacon and onions in skillet until onions are soft. Place onion mixture in large kettle; add reserved clam liquid, water, tomatoes, carrots, celery, thyme and pepper. Cook over low heat for 30 minutes. Dice clams; add clams and potatoes to tomato mixture. Cook until potatoes are tender. Yield: 8-10 servings.

Mrs. Evelyn Grabowski
Plant City, Florida

FISH GUMBO

1 lb. frozen fish fillets
1/3 c. butter
2 lge. onions, chopped
2 green peppers, chopped
2 No. 2 cans tomatoes and okra
2 tsp. salt
1/4 tsp. pepper
1 bay leaf
1 c. cooked rice

Thaw fillets on bottom shelf of refrigerator or at room temperature. Melt butter in saucepan; add onions and peppers. Cook until tender. Stir in tomatoes and okra and seasonings. Cook over low heat for at least 15 minutes. Cut fish fillets into cubes. Add fish and rice to gumbo. Cook for about 8 minutes or until fish flakes easily when tested with fork. Serve immediately. Yield: 4 servings.

EASY OYSTER STEW

4 c. milk
1/2 c. margarine
1/2 tsp. salt
1/2 tsp. celery salt
12 saltine crackers
1 pt. oysters

Scald milk in heavy saucepan; add margarine and seasonings. Stir until margarine is melted. Crush crackers to fine crumbs; stir into hot milk mixture. Add oysters; cook only until edges of oysters curl.

Mrs. Frances Blount
Birmingham, Alabama

CREAMY OYSTER STEW

1 pt. oysters, undrained
5 tbsp. butter or margarine
1 c. cream
3 c. milk, scalded
1/2 tsp. salt
Pepper to taste
Paprika to taste

Combine oysters and 3 tablespoons butter in heavy saucepan; cook until edge of oysters curl. Stir in cream and milk; heat almost to a boil. Add salt and pepper. Sprinkle with paprika; place remaining butter on top. Serve immediately. Yield: 4 servings.

Iona Ross
Freer, Texas

BURR'S FISH CHOWDER

2 lb. sea bass
1 qt. diced potatoes
1/4 lb. salt pork, diced
2 med. onions, chopped
1/4 c. flour
1 c. strained tomatoes
Salt and pepper to taste
Cayenne pepper to taste
Dash of hot sauce
Chopped parsley

Cut bass into 2-inch pieces; place in saucepan. Add 1 quart water. Cook until tender; drain, reserving liquid. Cook potatoes in 1 quart water; drain, reserving liquid. Fry salt pork and onions until lightly browned; cover. Cook for 10 minutes. Blend in flour; add reserved liquids slowly. Stir to a boil. Add tomatoes, bass and potatoes; mix lightly. Season with salt, pepper, cayenne pepper and hot sauce; sprinkle with parsley.

Mrs. Doris Burr
Hayward, California

NEW ORLEANS SALMON CHOWDER

1 1-lb. can salmon
1 bouillon cube
3/4 c. chopped onion
1/2 c. chopped green pepper
1 clove of garlic
1/4 c. butter
1 1-lb. can tomatoes
1 8-oz. can whole kernel corn
1/2 tsp. salt
1/4 tsp. thyme
Dash of pepper

Drain salmon, reserving 1/3 cup liquid. Break salmon into chunks. Dissolve bouillon cube in 1 cup boiling water. Cook onion, green pepper and garlic until tender in butter in large heavy saucepan. Add bouillon, reserved salmon liquid, tomatoes, corn and seasonings; mix well. Add salmon; simmer for 15 minutes. Serve with warm buttered saltines if desired.

Helen Janis Hale
Somerset, Kentucky

MICROWAVE SALMON AND DUMPLINGS

1 8-ct. can refrigerator biscuits
1 7-oz. can salmon
1 can Cheddar cheese soup
1 c. milk
2 tbsp. flour
2 tbsp. chopped green bell pepper
1 tbsp. chopped parsley

Arrange biscuits in bottom of 1 1/2-quart glass dish. Combine salmon, soup, milk, flour, green pepper and parsley in bowl; mix well. Spoon over biscuits. Microwave on High for 12 minutes, spooning sauce over biscuits again after 6 minutes.

Marilyn L. Burrows
Oklahoma City, Oklahoma

CHILI MAC

1/2 lb. ground beef
1 sm. onion, chopped
1/2 med. green pepper, chopped
Cooking oil
1 c. macaroni

1 8-oz. can kidney beans, undrained
1 8-oz. can tomato sauce
1/2 c. water
1/2 tsp. chili powder
1/2 tsp. salt
1/2 c. shredded Cheddar cheese

Brown ground beef, onion and green pepper in small amount of oil in large heavy skillet. Drain off fat; add macaroni, kidney beans, tomato sauce, water, chili powder and salt to skillet. Cover; simmer for 15 minutes, stirring occasionally. Top with cheese; heat until cheese is melted. Yield: 2-3 servings.

Mrs. Nancy S. Claibourne
Batavia, Ohio

CHILI WITH BEANS

2 tbsp. butter
1 1/2 c. diced onions
1 sm. clove of garlic
1 lb. ground beef
2 tbsp. chili powder
2 c. canned tomatoes
2 tsp. salt
1 tsp. sugar
4 c. cooked red kidney beans

Melt butter in saucepan. Add onions and garlic; cook until onions are tender. Do not brown. Add ground beef; cook, stirring, until beef is lightly browned. Mix chili powder to a paste with 2 tablespoons cold water; stir into ground beef mixture. Add tomatoes, salt and sugar; mix well. Bring to a boil; cover. Reduce heat; simmer for 1 hour. Add beans; cook until heated through.

Mrs. Peggy Hendrickson
Fourmile, Kentucky

CHILI POT

6 tbsp. butter or margarine
5 med. onions, sliced
3 lb. ground beef
2 tbsp. chili powder
1 tbsp. salt

1 tsp. paprika
3/4 tsp. hot sauce
2 1-lb. 12-oz. cans tomatoes
1 6-oz. can tomato paste
3 20-oz. cans kidney beans

Melt butter in 6 to 8-quart saucepan; add onions. Cook until tender but not brown. Add ground beef; sprinkle with chili powder, salt, paprika and hot sauce. Cook until ground beef is brown, breaking up with fork. Add tomatoes and tomato paste; cover. Simmer for 45 minutes. Add kidney beans; simmer for 15 minutes longer.

FREEZING CHILI

Freeze chili in ice cube trays; transfer to plastic bag for storage. Select needed number; thaw. Heat in saucepan.

Mrs. Raymond Moore
Alden, Iowa

POPPY SEED KRAUT AND WIENER GOULASH

12 frankfurters, cut in thirds
1/2 c. diced celery
1/4 c. butter or margarine
1 1/2 c. water
1 beef bouillon cube
1/2 tsp. salt
Dash of pepper
2 whole cloves
1 bay leaf
1/4 tsp. liquid gravy base
3 1/2 c. sauerkraut
1 to 1 1/2 tbsp. flour
1 1-lb. can sm. whole potatoes
1 1-lb. can sm. whole carrots
1 8-oz. can sm. whole onions
1 tsp. poppy seed

Cook frankfurters and celery in 2 tablespoons butter for about 3 minutes or until lightly browned. Mix in water, bouillon cube, seasonings and gravy base. Bring to a boil; boil gently for 10 minutes. Drain sauerkraut; reserve 1/4 cup liquid. Blend flour into reserved liquid; stir into boiling mixture. Cook for 1 minute, stirring constantly. Drain potatoes, carrots and onions; add to frankfurter mixture. Heat to serving temperature. Heat sauerkraut in saucepan in remaining butter; toss with poppy seed. Turn stew into serving dish; surround with sauerkraut mixture. Yield: 6 servings.

SESAME PASTRY-TOPPED STEW

1 tbsp. minced onion
1/2 tsp. dry oregano leaves
1/2 10-oz. package pie crust mix
1 1-lb. 14-oz. can meatball stew
1 egg white
1 tbsp. sesame seed

Preheat oven to 400 degrees. Add onion and oregano to dry pastry mix. Prepare pastry according to package directions. Roll out dough on lightly floured board. Cut into eight 2-inch long ovals. Place meatball stew into 6 x 10-inch baking dish. Bake for 10 minutes. Beat egg white until frothy. Spread each pastry oval with egg white. Sprinkle sesame seed over top of pastry. Remove stew from oven. Place pastry ovals on top of stew. Return to oven; bake for 15 minutes longer.

Mrs. Joe King
Los Angeles, California

BEEF STEW

2 lb. lean beef cubes
2 tbsp. flour
2 tbsp. shortening
2 c. water
1 can tomato sauce
2 tsp. salt
1/4 tsp. pepper
6 onions, chopped
6 carrots, chopped
6 potatoes, chopped
1 c. green peas

Roll beef in flour; brown beef in shortening in heavy saucepan. Add water, tomato sauce and seasonings. Cover tightly; cook over low heat for 1 hour and 30 minutes. Add onions, carrots and potatoes; cook for 30 minutes.

Add peas; cook until peas are tender. Yield: 6 servings.

Les V. Edmonds
Franklin, Louisiana

IRISH STEW

2 lb. stewing lamb
1/2 c. diced carrots
1/2 c. diced turnip
1 onion, sliced
1 potato, diced
2 c. sliced potatoes
Salt and pepper to taste

Cut lamb into 1-inch pieces; place in heavy kettle. Add enough boiling water to cover. Cover kettle; simmer for 1 hour. Add carrots, turnip, onion and diced potato; simmer for 30 minutes. Add sliced potatoes and seasonings; simmer for 30 minutes longer. Yield: 6 servings.

Mrs. Rebecca B. Sish
Pensacola, Florida

USE PRESSURE SAUCEPAN TO SAVE TIME AND MONEY

Save time by cooking vegetables in 5 to 10 minutes. Save money by buying less expensive cuts of meat. Cook chunks of beef chuck or round in pressure saucepan with beef bouillon as liquid for a flavorful stew without adding onions or strong seasonings.

Mrs. Delores Sorensen
Shiocton, Wisconsin

SAVORY STEW

3 lb. potatoes
1 5-lb. chicken
3 No. 2 cans tomatoes
1 8-oz. can tomato paste
2 No. 2 cans okra
2 No. 2 cans corn
3 lge. onions, diced
Salt to taste
Crushed red pepper to taste
1/2 c. margarine

Peel potatoes; cut in small pieces. Place potatoes in saucepan; add water to cover. Cook until potatoes are tender. Mash potatoes; do not drain. Place chicken in large kettle; add about 3 quarts water. Cook until chicken is tender. Strip chicken from bones; return to broth. Add tomatoes, tomato paste, okra, corn, onions and seasonings; mix well. Simmer, stirring frequently, for about 2 hours. Stir in potatoes and margarine; add water if needed. Cook for 15 minutes longer, stirring constantly.

Mrs. E. C. Henry
Canton, Mississippi

VEAL STEW WITH DUMPLINGS

2 lb. veal shoulder
1 onion, sliced
2 3/4 tsp. salt
1/4 tsp. pepper
1/2 tsp. Worcestershire sauce
2 c. diced potatoes
6 carrots, diced
1 3/4 c. flour
3 tsp. baking powder
2 tbsp. shortening
3/4 c. milk
Chopped parsley

Cut veal into 1-inch cubes; place in heavy kettle. Add onion and 4 cups water; simmer for 1 hour. Add 2 teaspoons salt, pepper, Worcestershire sauce, potatoes and carrots. Mix well; simmer until carrots are tender. Blend 1/4 cup flour to a paste with 1/4 cup cold water; stir into stew to thicken. Sift remaining flour, remaining salt and baking powder together into bowl; cut in shortening. Add milk; mix lightly. Drop dough from teaspoon into hot stew. Cover tightly; cook for 12 minutes. Sprinkle with parsley before serving. Yield: 6-8 servings.

Anita Smith
Edinburg, Texas

Meat, Poultry, & Seafood

When budget-minded homemakers want to serve their families low-cost, nutritious, and delicious dinners, they turn to thrifty cuts of meat, poultry, and seafood for help. Over years of planning economical yet family-pleasing meals, these women have developed and perfected a wide range of recipes using inexpensive cuts of meat, low-cost fish and seafood, and that all-time money-saver, poultry.

In the following section, you'll discover recipes that help you turn every meal into a delightful adventure for your family. Here are the thoughtful recipes that use special cooking methods and just the right touch of herbs and spices to turn low-cost meats, fish, and poultry into adventures in good eating. Even chops and roasts – once thought to be expensive – can fit into the tightest budget using the hints and recipes in the following pages. Here, too, you'll find wonderful recipes using poultry – everything from a quick barbecue to an elegant, party-perfect dinner – and fresh, canned, and frozen fish and seafood.

Accompanying the recipes are budget-saving hints and tricks from America's thriftiest homemakers – just what you need to get even more for your money!

Meat, Poultry, & Seafood

GETTING MORE FOR YOUR MONEY

MEAT

Meat that travels between states must be inspected by the U. S. Department of Agriculture. *U. S. Prime* is the very best rating. *U. S. Choice* is high-quality meat with smooth texture and white fat marbling. It and *U. S. Good* are the grades you're most apt to find. The other grade you'll probably find is *U. S. Commercial* – good for stewing but not much else.

Beef is most often quality rated. Other meats must be judged on their appearance. In *veal,* look for fine texture and firm flesh, light greyish-pink in color, with little fat marbling.

Lamb should be firm and fine-grained with pink or white fat. Lamb is another hard-to-find meat, but Italian and Greek grocery stores will have ample supplies of top-quality lamb – and at lower than supermarket prices.

Pork should have light greyish-pink flesh, fine grained with a layer of firm white fat. Good pork is available year-round in grocery stores. The Germans love fine pork and ham – and a German butcher will probably have the very best quality pork at low prices.

Most top cooks recommend you deal directly with the butcher. When you buy packaged meats, you have no way of getting the trimmed-off fat and bones you need for your stockpot, you lose flavor and juices because these are absorbed by the paper layer in most packages, and you run the risk of buying what appears to be good meat only to find out that it's a poorer grade on the bottom.

POULTRY

Chicken is in plentiful supply year-round, but the prices are lowest when huge numbers of chickens appear on the market. When shopping for a chicken, look for birds with short, plump bodies and a good fatty layer. The skin should show no bruises, pin feathers, or discoloration. If the chickens are pre-packaged, the packages should be unbroken. Almost all poultry sold is Grade A. Under the latest legislation, chicken-packing plants are continuously inspected for your family's protection.

Broiler-fryers are in good supply from May to September. A cut-up chicken will be a few cents per pound more than a whole one – if you buy in quantity, you'll realize a big savings by cutting chicken up yourself. Allow about one-half a chicken per person.

Roasting chickens are in plentiful supply from September to January. The average roaster weighs between three and five pounds – count on three-fourths of a pound per person. Roasters are lower in price than broiler-fryers.

Lowest priced of all are stewing hens. These tough birds weigh between three and eight pounds and are an excellent value, especially between October and January.

Turkeys are a wonderful buy, particularly at the end of November and late in December. The most economical buy is a large turkey – between 16 and 20 pounds. If it is too big for you to use, ask your butcher to cut it in half. You cook half now and keep the other half in your freezer until you need it. A 16- to 20-pound turkey will yield enough meat to serve a family of four for six meals. At a price of 89 cents a pound, that works out to a little more than 2 dollars per meal – a wonderful bargain for you and delicious eating for your family.

SEAFOOD

Fresh fish may be whole, dressed (cleaned and scaled), or cut into steaks or fillets. When shopping for fresh fish, look for a fresh, mild odor; bright, clear, and full eyes; gills that are red and free of slime; shining, iridescent skin; and firm, elastic flesh. When you touch the flesh, it should not retain your fingerprint but should spring back. Fish with a white, cotton-like appearance, a brownish tinge, or discoloration in the flesh is of poor quality.

Frozen fish should be carefully packaged with almost all the air gone from the package. If a "fishy" odor is present, the fish is not good. If the fish is packaged in clear wrap and you detect any of the signs listed in the previous paragraph, then the fish should not be purchased.

Fresh clams and oysters bought in the shell should have their shells unbroken and tightly closed. Both clam and oyster meat may be removed from the shell and sold separately – both should have a natural cream color and be surrounded by clear liquid. Crabs and lobsters taste best when bought alive and kept that way until they are cooked. Scallops are available in two varieties – tender bay scallops and the tougher ocean ones. Fresh scallop meat has a sweetish odor, no liquid, and is a creamy white color. Fresh shrimp should have a clean shell tightly attached to their bodies.

Several types of frozen shellfish are available breaded and ready for frying. But you'll get more for your money if you buy fresh or frozen shellfish and bread them yourself.

BARBECUED SHORT RIBS

3 lb. short ribs
1 onion, chopped
1/4 c. vinegar
2 tbsp. sugar
2 tsp. salt
1 c. catsup
1/2 c. water
3 tbsp. Worcestershire sauce
1 tsp. prepared mustard
1/2 c. sliced celery

Cut ribs into serving pieces; brown ribs and onion in 2 tablespoons hot fat in skillet. Combine remaining ingredients; add to ribs. Cover; cook over low heat for 1 hour and 30 minutes to 2 hours or until tender.

Mrs. Della O. Lindsay
Broadman, Oregon

BARBECUED POT ROAST

1 3 to 4-lb. arm or blade beef roast
Meat tenderizer
1/2 c. barbecue sauce
2 tbsp. soy sauce
1 tbsp. Worcestershire sauce
1/2 clove of garlic, minced
Dash of basil
Dash of oregano
Dash of crushed thyme

Sprinkle beef with meat tenderizer according to label directions; place in Dutch oven. Combine remaining ingredients; pour over beef. Cover pan tightly. Bake at 325 degrees for 3 hours or until beef is tender. Make gravy from pan drippings if desired.

Mrs. Jessye P. MacKay
Pollack, South Dakota

FRUITED POT ROAST

1 3 to 4-lb. pot roast
Salt and pepper to taste
1 c. apple cider
2 tbsp. sugar
1/4 tsp. cinnamon
1/4 tsp. ginger
3 whole cloves
1 1/2 c. sliced onions
12 dried apricots
12 prunes

Brown roast on all sides in small amount of hot fat in roaster; season with salt and pepper. Combine apple cider, sugar, cinnamon, ginger and cloves; pour over roast. Add onions. Cover; simmer for 2 hours or until roast is tender. Soak dried apricots and prunes in water to cover until plump. Drain fruits; let stand for 30 minutes. Add to roast. Bake for 30 minutes longer. Thicken pan liquid for gravy if desired. Yield: 6-8 servings.

Mrs. Nancy Jones
Bardwell, Kentucky

SELECTING REDUCED PRICE BEEF PACKAGES

Watch for reduced price packages in which meat is beginning to look brown, when shopping for beef. Brown color indicates aging which tenderizes and adds to flavor. These beef packages are often reduced in price because many people do not realize that exposure to lights in meat cases causes slight loss of bright color.

Ruth Riffe
Hobart, Oklahoma

PEPPER STEAK

1 2-lb. round steak
1 clove of garlic, halved
Salt
Pepper to taste
1/4 c. flour
3 tbsp. oil
1 6-oz. can tomato paste
1 1/2 c. water
1 bay leaf
1/4 tsp. thyme

1 lge. onion, sliced
1 green pepper, cut into rings

Cut steak into serving pieces. Rub with garlic; sprinkle with salt to taste and pepper. Pound flour into steak. Heat oil in large skillet; brown steak well on both sides. Place steak in casserole. Drain oil from skillet. Mix tomato paste, water, 1/2 teaspoon salt, bay leaf and thyme; heat in same skillet. Arrange onion and green pepper rings over steak; pour tomato mixture over all. Cover tightly. Bake at 350 degrees for 1 hour to 1 hour and 30 minutes. Yield: 6 servings.

Mrs. Jewell Spivey
Gilmer, Texas

IDEA FOR BAKING GREEN PEPPERS

Arrange stuffed green peppers in greased muffin tins to bake.

Karenann Manley
Granby, Colorado

STUFFED GREEN PEPPERS

6 lge. green peppers
1 lb. ground beef
1 c. dry bread crumbs
1 tsp. salt
1/4 tsp. pepper
1 tbsp. chopped onion
1 1/2 c. tomato juice

Remove stems and seeds from green peppers. Rinse and drain on paper towel. Mix ground beef, bread crumbs, salt, pepper, onion and 1/2 cup tomato juice. Stuff green peppers with beef mixture. Place in 1 1/2-quart baking dish. Pour remaining tomato juice over stuffed peppers. Bake, covered, at 350 degrees for 45 minutes. Uncover; bake for 15 minutes longer. Yield: 6 servings.

Ann Holman
Alexandria, Pennsylvania

GIANT HAMBURGER WITH APPLE BARBECUE SAUCE

1 c. bottled barbecue sauce
2 c. applesauce
2 tbsp. lemon juice
2 lb. ground beef
2 eggs
1/2 c. chopped onion
1/4 c. minced parsley
1 c. seasoned bread crumbs
1 tbsp. salt
1 tsp. dry mustard
1/2 lb. sliced bacon

Combine barbecue sauce, 1 cup applesauce and lemon juice for sauce. Combine remaining applesauce with remaining ingredients except bacon; mix thoroughly. Turn onto heavy-duty foil; shape into large flat cake about 1 1/2 inches thick. Secure bacon slices around meat cake with skewers; arrange remaining slices on top. Place meat on foil in shallow roasting pan. Bake at 400 degrees for about 45 to 50 minutes, basting frequently with sauce. Serve hot with any remaining sauce. Cut in wedges to serve. Sprinkle wedges with blue cheese curls if desired. Yield: 8-10 servings.

EASY ECONOMICAL MEAT LOAVES

2 lb. ground beef
1 lb. ground ham
2 c. oats
1 c. bread crumbs
3 eggs
1 c. milk
1 sm. ground onion
2 tsp. salt
1/4 tsp. pepper
1 1/2 qt. tomato juice

Combine all ingredients except 1 quart tomato juice; form into loaves. Place in deep baking dish. Add remaining tomato juice. Bake at 325 degrees for 2 hours. Yield: 20 servings.

Mrs. Frances Detmer
Weeping Water, Nebraska

ITALIAN SPAGHETTI WITH MEATBALLS

1 med. onion, chopped
2 cloves of garlic, minced
2 tbsp. cooking oil
1 pt. tomatoes, mashed
1 6-oz. can tomato paste
4 tsp. oregano
2 tsp. salt
1/4 tsp. pepper
1 lb. ground beef
4 slices bacon
2 hard-cooked eggs, chopped
1 slice bread, diced
8 oz. spaghetti
Grated Parmesan cheese

Saute onion and garlic in oil in large skillet. Add tomatoes, tomato paste, 3 teaspoons oregano, 1 teaspoon salt and pepper. Simmer for 1 hour and 30 minutes to 2 hours or until thick. Combine beef, remaining salt and remaining oregano. Fry bacon; drain, reserving drippings. Crumble bacon. Combine eggs, bread, bacon and 2 tablespoons reserved drippings; form into balls. Press beef mixture firmly around egg balls. Fry in remaining bacon drippings for 10 minutes. Add meatballs to tomato sauce; simmer for 10 minutes longer. Cook spaghetti in boiling salted water for 7 minutes or until tender; drain. Spread spaghetti on serving platter. Cover with meatballs and sauce; sprinkle with cheese. Yield: 6 servings.

Mrs. Velma Cain
Burwell, Nebraska

HOBO DINNER

1 lb. ground beef
2 med. potatoes, quartered
2 med. onions, quartered
2 carrots, sliced
2 tbsp. butter
Salt and pepper to taste

Shape beef into 2 patties; place on sheet of aluminum foil. Top with potatoes, onions and carrots; wrap tightly. Bake at 350 degrees for 1 hour. Season patties and vegetables with butter, salt and pepper; serve immediately. Yield: 2 servings.

Jean Bugg
Highland Home, Alabama

TWICE AROUND HAMBURGER

Cut leftover hamburgers or meat loaf into small pieces. Combine one 15-ounce can tomato sauce, hamburgers, 1 teaspoon chopped onion and 2 tablespoons butter in saucepan; heat through. Cook 8 ounces thin spaghetti according to package directions. Drain spaghetti and add to sauce. Mix well and pour into 2-quart casserole. Top with grated cheese. Bake in 350-degree oven for 15 to 20 minutes. This is an economical and nourishing meal for 4 to 6 people.

Sister Vincent Louise
Hempstead, New York

EASY MICROWAVE LASAGNA

8 oz. ground beef
1 32-oz. jar spaghetti sauce
1 1/2 c. ricotta cheese
1 egg
1/2 tsp. pepper
8 uncooked lasagna noodles
2 c. shredded mozzarella cheese
1/2 c. Parmesan cheese

Crumble ground beef into microwave-safe colander in glass bowl. Microwave on High for 4 minutes or until no longer pink, stirring once. Combine with spaghetti sauce and 1/2 cup water in bowl; mix well. Spread 1/2 cup meat sauce in shallow glass dish. Mix ricotta cheese, egg and pepper in bowl. Layer uncooked noodles, ricotta mixture, mozzarella cheese and remaining meat sauce 1/2 at a time in prepared dish. Wrap tightly with plastic wrap. Microwave on Medium-Low for 30 to 32 minutes or until noodles are tender. Sprinkle with Parmesan cheese.

Suzanne Phister
Princeton, Missouri

T-BONE STEAKETTES

4 slices stale bread
1 lb. hamburger
3/4 c. tomato juice
1/4 c. catsup
2 tbsp. minced onion
1 tsp. salt
1/2 tsp. pepper
1 egg, beaten
Thin carrot strips

Place bread in deep bowl; cover with cold water. Let stand for 1 hour; squeeze bread dry, crumbling well. Combine hamburger, tomato juice, catsup, onion, salt, pepper, egg and bread crumbs; mix well. Shape mixture to resemble small steaks, using carrot strips for bones. Place on broiler pan. Broil for 10 minutes on each side or until browned.

Mrs. Louise H. Motes
Laurens, South Carolina

ADAPTING RECIPES FOR THE MICROWAVE

To adapt your favorite meat loaf recipes for the microwave, increase the dry filler by 1/4 cup for each 1 1/2 pounds of ground beef; decrease the liquid by 1/2 if the filler is soft bread crumbs.

Wilma Morris
Houston, Texas

SALISBURY STEAK

1 egg
1/2 c. milk
2 slices soft bread, crumbled
1 lb. lean ground beef
1 1/2 tsp. salt
1/2 tsp. pepper
1/2 tsp. paprika
1/4 c. minced green pepper
1/4 c. minced celery
1/4 c. minced onion
1 c. dry bread crumbs
Cooking oil

Beat egg; add milk and bread. Let stand for about 10 minutes. Add beef, seasonings, green pepper, celery and onion; mix well. Shape beef mixture in 1/2-inch thick patties; coat patties with dry bread crumbs. Heat about 1/4 inch oil in skillet. Add beef patties; cook until browned on both sides.

Mrs. Vada Belle Zellner
San Antonio, Texas

FREEZING AND THAWING GROUND BEEF PATTIES

Shape ground beef into 1/4-pound patties and place between sheets of waxed paper. Freeze and place in plastic bags to store in freezer. Patties thaw much faster than a solid chunk of beef.

Mrs. Janet Dersey
Livonia, Michigan

MICROWAVE SWEET AND SOUR PORK

1 8-oz. can pineapple chunks
2 tbsp. brown sugar
2 tbsp. cornstarch
1/4 c. teriyaki sauce
3 tbsp. cider vinegar
1 1/2 tsp. catsup
1 lb. boneless pork shoulder
2 med. green bell peppers

Drain pineapple, reserving juice. Mix brown sugar and cornstarch in glass dish. Blend in reserved pineapple juice, teriyaki sauce, vinegar and catsup. Cut pork and green pepper into 3/4-inch pieces. Add to sauce. Microwave, covered, on High for 5 minutes. Stir in pineapple. Microwave, covered, on Medium for 12 to 15 minutes or until pork is cooked through, stirring once. Serve over rice.

Joyce Foltz
Brigham City, Utah

USE THE RIGHT MICROWAVE DISH

Avoid using baking dishes with sloping sides in the microwave because food on the edges receives the most energy and may overcook. Stir foods from the outside toward the center to equalize the temperature.

Haley Stephenson
Winchester, Kentucky

BAKED LEMON PORK CHOPS

1/2 tsp. salt
1/8 tsp. pepper
1 c. flour
3 or 4 thick lean loin chops
Shortening
3 or 4 slices lemon
1/2 c. catsup
1/2 c. water
1 1/2 tbsp. brown sugar

Combine salt, pepper and flour; dredge chops in seasoned flour. Brown on both sides in small amount of shortening. Arrange chops in baking dish. Place 1 lemon slice on each chop. Mix catsup, water and brown sugar together. Pour over chops. Bake, uncovered, at 350 degrees for 45 minutes to 1 hour or until done, adding small amount of water if needed. Yield: 3-4 servings.

Barbara Waybourn
Afton, Texas

PORK SURPRISE

4 lge. lean pork chops
Salad oil
4 thick slices onion
1/2 can cream of mushroom soup
1/4 c. milk
1/4 c. peanut butter
1 tsp. Worcestershire sauce
1 tsp. salt
1/8 tsp. pepper

Brown chops on both sides in small amount of oil in large skillet; pour off fat. Place onion slices on chops. Blend soup and milk; add peanut butter, Worcestershire sauce and seasonings. Mix well; pour over chops. Cover skillet. Cook over low heat for 45 minutes.

Nettie-Adelyn Landau
Fallon, Nevada

STUFFED HAM SLICES

2 ham slices, 1/2 in. thick
1/4 c. chopped celery
2 tbsp. chopped parsley
1/4 c. butter
1 12-oz. can crushed pineapple
4 c. dry bread cubes
1/2 tsp. ground marjoram
1 1/2 tsp. lemon juice
Dash of ground cloves

Place 1 ham slice in baking pan; set aside. Cook celery and parsley in butter until tender. Add 3/4 cup pineapple, bread cubes and marjoram; mix well. Spoon bread crumb mixture over ham slice. Place remaining ham slice over bread crumb mixture. Combine remaining pineapple, lemon juice and cloves; spread over top. Pour small amount of water into baking pan. Bake at 325 degrees for 1 hour. Yield: 6 servings.

Mrs. Cora Ann Coleman
Coffeeville, Alabama

HAM LOAF AND RAISIN SAUCE

1 1/2 lb. ground smoked ham
2 lb. ground fresh pork
1 c. milk
1 c. cracker crumbs
1 c. tomato juice
2 tbsp. flour
2 tbsp. butter
1 c. apple cider or fruit juice
2 tbsp. brown sugar
1/4 c. raisins
1/8 tsp. salt

Combine ham, pork, milk, crumbs and tomato juice; shape into loaf. Place in 7 x 10-inch baking pan. Bake at 325 degrees for 1 hour and 40 minutes. Combine flour and butter; add cider gradually, stirring constantly. Add remaining ingredients; mix well. Spread over ham loaf. Bake for 20 minutes longer. Slices of pineapple may be arranged on loaf just before loaf is done if desired.

Mrs. Theresa H. Smith
Warner Robins, Georgia

HAM-SOMES

2 c. sifted flour
3 1/2 tsp. baking powder
1/2 tsp. salt
2 tsp. sugar
1/2 c. shortening
2 tsp. caraway seed
2 eggs
Milk
2 1/2 c. ground cooked ham
1 onion, ground
2 tbsp. chopped parsley
1 tbsp. prepared horseradish
2 tsp. dry mustard
1/8 tsp. pepper

Sift flour, baking powder, salt and sugar together. Cut in shortening until particles resemble coarse cornmeal; stir in caraway seed. Beat 1 egg; add enough milk to make 2/3 cup mixture. Add to dry ingredients all at once. Stir until dough forms ball. Knead gently on floured surface. Roll out to 12 x 10-inch rectangle. Beat remaining egg; combine with remaining ingredients. Mix thoroughly. Spread mixture evenly over dough. Roll as for jelly roll, starting with 12-inch side. Cut into eight slices; place, cut side down, 1 inch apart on ungreased baking sheet. Bake at 425 degrees for 15 to 20 minutes. Yield: 8 servings.

Mrs. Virginia O. Sheely
Littlestown, Pennsylvania

GLAZED HAM BALLS

1/2 lb. ground ham
3/4 lb. ground pork
2/3 c. oats
1 egg, beaten
1/2 c. milk
1/3 c. brown sugar
2 tbsp. flour
1 tsp. dry mustard
2/3 c. fruit juice
2 tbsp. vinegar
6 whole cloves
1/3 c. dark syrup

Combine ham, pork, oats, egg and milk; mix well. Chill thoroughly. Shape into small balls; place in shallow baking pan. Bake at 300 degrees for 1 hour. Drain. Combine remaining ingredients in saucepan; cook over medium heat until slightly thickened. Pour over ham balls. Bake for 15 minutes longer.

Josephine Tupy
New Prague, Minnesota

SAUSAGE BALLS

2 lb. bulk sausage
1 med. onion, diced
2 qt. water
1 46-oz. can tomato juice
1 lge. package noodles

Shape sausage into 1-inch balls. Combine onion and water in large kettle; bring to a boil. Drop in sausage balls. Cover; reduce heat. Simmer for 15 minutes. Chill for several hours or overnight. Skim fat from sausage broth; add tomato juice. Bring to a boil. Add noodles; cook until noodles are tender. Yield: 8 servings.

Mrs. Mary Kathryn Lands
Amanda, Ohio

BROILED LAMB WITH VEGETABLES

2 tbsp. chopped onion
1 tbsp. lard
2 c. cooked rice
1 c. tomato juice
Dash of salt
Dash of pepper
1 No. 2 can string beans, drained
6 shoulder lamb chops

Brown onion in lard in skillet; add rice, tomato juice and seasonings. Heat through. Place rice mixture in middle of bottom of broiler pan. Place beans around edge. Arrange lamb chops on rack over rice mixture. Broil for 10 minutes on each side. Yield: 4-6 servings.

Shirley Humphrey
Albin, Wyoming

RAISIN-LAMB CURRY

1 tbsp. curry powder
1 tbsp. butter
1 med. onion, sliced
2 med. stalks celery, sliced
1 1/2 lb. cubed lean lamb
1 14-oz. can chicken broth
1 tsp. garlic salt
1 1/2 tbsp. cornstarch
2/3 c. seedless raisins
Persian Rice

Combine curry powder, butter, onion and celery in large saucepan; cover. Cook over moderate heat for several minutes or until vegetables are wilted. Add lamb, broth and salt. Cover tightly; simmer for 1 hour to 1 hour and 30 minutes or until lamb is tender. Combine cornstarch with 2 tablespoons water; stir into lamb mixture. Add raisins. Cook slowly for 15 minutes longer, stirring frequently. Serve with Persian Rice.

Persian Rice

2 tbsp. butter
1 c. rice
1 c. orange juice
1 tsp. salt
1/2 c. seedless raisins
1/4 c. slivered toasted almonds
1/4 tsp. grated orange peel
1 tbsp. chopped parsley

Combine butter and rice in skillet; cook, stirring, over moderate heat until lightly toasted. Stir in orange juice, 1 1/2 cups water, salt and raisins. Cover tightly; simmer over low heat for about 15 minutes, until rice has absorbed all liquid and is tender. Stir once or twice during first 5 minutes of cooking. Remove from heat; fluff rice with fork. Add almonds, orange peel and parsley.

Photograph for this recipe on page 46.

LAMB CHOPS DELUXE

6 3/4-in. thick lamb chops
3 tbsp. shortening
1 1/2 tsp. salt
1/4 tsp. pepper
1 tsp. garlic salt
1 tsp. paprika
1/2 tsp. nutmeg

Brown chops on both sides in shortening in skillet. Combine seasonings; sprinkle on both sides of chops. Pour off drippings. Cover; cook over low heat until tender and done, adding liquid if necessary. Yield: 6 servings.

Mrs. Sally A. Kmon
Manchester, New Hampshire

RICH BROWN GRAVY HINT

To deepen color of gravy stir in a small amount of instant coffee.

Mrs. Mary E. Cantwell
West Winfield, New York

FAVORITE BARBECUED CHICKEN

1/2 c. salad oil
1/2 c. tomato sauce
1/2 c. red wine
1 tsp. salt
1 tsp. sugar
1 tbsp. Worcestershire sauce
2 to 3 drops of liquid smoke
2 lge. cloves of garlic, minced
1 tsp. dry mustard
Dash of pepper
2 chickens

Combine first 10 ingredients in order listed in jar. Cover and refrigerate overnight. Marinate chicken in sauce for 4 to 5 hours, stirring occasionally. Drain and reserve marinade. Grill chicken for 1 hour to 1 hour and 30 minutes over medium coals. Turn; baste often with reserved marinade.

Mrs. Joanne Litz
Tulare, California

DELICIOUS OVEN-BARBECUED CHICKEN

3/4 c. chopped onion
1/2 c. margarine
3/4 c. catsup
1/3 c. lemon juice or vinegar
3 tbsp. brown sugar
3 tbsp. Worcestershire sauce
2 tbsp. mustard
1 tsp. pepper
2 frying chickens, halved
Salt to taste

Saute onion in margarine in skillet; add catsup, 3/4 cup water, lemon juice, brown sugar, Worcestershire sauce, mustard and pepper. Cook for 15 minutes. Season chicken with salt; dip into sauce. Place chicken in baking pan. Bake at 350 degrees for 1 hour and 30 minutes. Baste with sauce several times while baking.

Mrs. Rozanne Aker
Waynetown, Indiana

MICROWAVE APRICOT CHICKEN

5 chicken breasts
1 tbsp. (heaping) mayonnaise
1/2 env. dry onion soup mix
1/4 c. Russian salad dressing
1/2 c. apricot preserves

Rinse chicken and pat dry. Arrange in shallow glass dish, placing thickest portions toward outer edge. Combine mayonnaise, onion soup mix, salad dressing and apricot preserves in bowl; mix well. Spread over chicken, covering completely. Microwave, covered, on High for 7 minutes per pound, turning dish once. Yield: 5 servings.

Carole Mayer
Des Moines, Iowa

MICROWAVING IN COOKING BAGS

Chicken is an especially good choice for cooking in a plastic cooking (not storage) bag in the microwave. Close the bag loosely with string or a plastic tie. For a brown surface, brush with bottled brown sauce diluted with water. Take care when removing chicken from bag to avoid steam burns.

Joanne Jacobs
Baltimore, Maryland

BUTTERED-GRILLED CHICKEN

1/2 c. butter, melted
2 tsp. lemon juice
1 2 to 3-lb. chicken, disjointed
Salt and pepper to taste

Combine butter and lemon juice. Brush chicken with lemon-butter; sprinkle with salt and pepper. Cook chicken on hot grill, 5 or 6 inches from briquettes for 10 minutes; turn and brush with lemon-butter. Cook for 20 to 30 minutes longer, turning and basting at 10-minute intervals. Yield: 4 servings.

LaVonne L. Wiener
Thornton, Iowa

ORANGE-GRILLED CHICKEN

Salt and pepper to taste
Poultry seasoning to taste
1/2 tsp. monosodium glutamate
1 sm. can frozen orange juice
1 2 1/2-lb. broiling chicken, halved
1/4 c. melted butter

Combine salt, pepper, poultry seasoning and monosodium glutamate; add orange juice. Grill chicken over low heat for about 1 hour, turning and basting with butter and orange juice mixture at 5 to 10-minute intervals.

Mrs. Kathryn Leischner
DeLand, Illinois

NEW-FASHIONED MICROWAVE CHICKEN

Prepare all your favorite chicken recipes in the microwave. For dishes that you prefer crisp and brown, just bake in your conventional oven at 450 degrees for 10 minutes after microwaving. For quick grilled chicken, microwave it until it is almost tender and then place it on the grill long enough to give it that good charcoal flavor. It's healthier, too!

Penny Stoneman
Birmingham, Alabama

CHICKEN CALIFORNIA

1 3 1/2-lb. broiler, cut up
2 tbsp. butter
2 tbsp. salad oil
1 can chicken broth
1/4 c. finely chopped onion
1 tbsp. vinegar
1 tsp. salt
1/4 tsp. pepper
3 tbsp. prepared Dijon mustard
2 tbsp. sugar
Flour
2 fresh Bartlett pears
1/2 c. dark seedless raisins

Wash and dry chicken; saute in large skillet in butter and salad oil until golden. Add chicken broth, 1 broth can water, onion, vinegar, salt and pepper to skillet. Mix mustard with sugar; stir into liquid in skillet. Cover tightly; simmer for 45 minutes or until chicken is fork-tender. Blend 1 or 2 tablespoons flour with equal amount of water; stir into skillet. Cook, stirring gently until thickened. Halve, core and quarter pears; add with raisins to chicken and sauce. Heat through. Yield: 4 servings.

MICROWAVE CHICKEN FIESTA

4 chicken breast filets
3 tbsp. butter, softened
2 tbsp. sharp cheese spread, softened
2 tsp. onion flakes
1 tsp. salt
2 tbsp. chopped green chilies
2/3 c. melted butter
1 1/2 c. cheese cracker crumbs
2 1/2 tbsp. taco seasoning mix

Rinse chicken and pat dry. Pound with meat mallet to flatten. Blend 3 tablespoons butter and cheese spread in bowl. Add onion flakes, salt and green chilies; mix well. Spoon onto chicken. Roll chicken to enclose filling; secure with toothpicks. Dip in melted butter; coat with mixture of cracker crumbs and

taco seasoning. Place in 2-quart glass dish. Microwave on High for 6 to 7 minutes, turning dish once. Yield: 4 servings.

Crystal Lee
Tacoma, Washington

MAMA'S GARLIC-FRIED CHICKEN

2 2 1/2-lb. fryers, disjointed
1 c. sour cream
2 tbsp. lemon juice
1/4 tsp. Worcestershire sauce
1 clove of garlic, grated
1/2 tsp. salt
1/4 tsp. pepper
1/4 tsp. celery salt
1/2 tsp. paprika
Flour

Wipe chicken with damp cloth. Place in large bowl. Mix remaining ingredients except flour; pour over chicken, covering all pieces well. Cover bowl tightly; refrigerate overnight. Drain; dredge with flour. Fry until done. Yield: 6 servings.

Mrs. Jim Hudson
Celeste, Texas

MICROWAVE TURKEY MEATBALLS

1 1/2 lb. ground turkey
1 1/2 tbsp. instant chicken bouillon
1 tsp. poultry seasoning
1/2 tsp. pepper
1/2 c. chopped parsley
1 c. chopped onion
1/2 c. chopped celery
1/4 c. margarine
1 c. milk
1 1/2 c. stuffing mix
1 can chicken-mushroom soup
1/2 c. sour cream

Combine ground turkey, chicken bouillon, poultry seasoning, pepper and parsley in bowl; mix well. Combine onion and celery with butter in large glass dish. Microwave on High for 2 minutes or until tender. Stir in milk. Microwave for 1 1/2 minutes or just until warm. Stir in stuffing mix. Add to turkey mixture; mix well. Shape into 1 1/2-inch meatballs. Place in glass dish. Microwave, loosely covered, on High for 7 minutes, turning meatballs once. Blend soup, sour cream and 1/4 cup water in dish. Microwave on High just until heated through. Pour over meatballs. Microwave on High for 4 minutes or until heated through. Yield: 4 servings.

Ruth Hinsch
El Paso, Texas

LEMON-BUTTERED HADDOCK

4 haddock fillets
Salt and pepper to taste
3/4 c. butter or margarine
3 lemons, sliced
3 med. onions, sliced

Place fillets on 4 large sheets of aluminum foil; season with salt and pepper. Spread 3 tablespoons butter over each fillet; top with lemons and onions. Fold foil over; seal ends. Place on hot coals. Cook for about 30 minutes, turning once. Yield: 4 servings.

Rosemarie Burns
Saugerties, New York

MICROWAVE SWEET AND SOUR FISH

1 lb. fish fillets
1 8-oz. can pineapple chunks
3 tbsp. brown sugar
1 tbsp. cornstarch
1/4 tbsp. dry mustard
2 tbsp. vinegar
1 tbsp. soy sauce
1 1/2 oz. cashews

Arrange fillets in shallow glass dish. Microwave, covered, on High for 5 minutes or until fish flakes easily; drain. Drain pineapple, reserving juice. Blend reserved juice with brown sugar, cornstarch, dry mustard, vinegar and soy sauce in glass dish. Microwave for 1 1/2 to 2 minutes or until thickened, stirring once. Stir in pineapple and cashews. Spoon over fillets. Microwave for 1 to 2 minutes or until heated through. Yield: 4 servings.

Rachel Paige
Flint, Michigan

CREAMED MUSHROOMS AND CRAB MEAT

1/3 c. butter
1/3 c. flour
2 c. sour cream
1 tbsp. dried onion flakes
1 tbsp. dried parsley flakes
1/4 tsp. nutmeg
1 lb. crab meat, drained
2 4-oz. cans mushrooms, drained
3 tbsp. sherry

Melt butter in saucepan over low heat; blend flour in until smooth. Stir in sour cream and remaining ingredients. Cover; cook for 25 to 30 minutes. Serve in rice ring if desired. Yield: 6-8 servings.

Mrs. Mildred R. Buck
Linden, Alabama

EGG FOO YUNG WITH CRAB

1/2 c. chopped onion
Oil
1/2 c. chopped tomatoes
1 pkg. frozen crab meat
3 eggs, beaten
Salt and pepper to taste
Monosodium glutamate to taste
2 tbsp. soy sauce
1 c. broth
1 tbsp. cornstarch

Saute onion lightly in about 1 tablespoon oil. Add tomatoes; simmer for 2 minutes. Add crab meat; cook until heated through. Stir in eggs, salt, pepper and monosodium glutamate; mix well. Shape crab meat mixture into patties; fry in oil in skillet until browned. Combine soy sauce and broth in saucepan; bring to a boil. Blend cornstarch to a paste with 1 tablespoon water; add to hot mixture. Cook until thickened; serve over crab meat patties.

Mrs. Wilma C. Mitchell
Smithville, Ohio

MICROWAVE TIPS FOR FISH

For even cooking, arrange fish fillets in a glass dish with the thickest portions toward the outside of the dish. Do not cover fish during microwaving if it has a breading on it. Otherwise, most fish dishes should be covered with vented plastic wrap to retain moisture.

Irene Dunlop
Ventura, California

OYSTER PIE

Pastry for 2-crust 9-in. pie
1 1/2 qt. medium oysters
Salt to taste
2 tbsp. flour

1/4 c. butter
1/2 tsp. hot sauce

Line 9-inch pie plate with half the pastry. Drain oysters, reserving 1/4 cup liquor. Turn oysters into pie pastry; sprinkle with salt and flour. Dot with butter. Combine reserved oyster liquor and hot sauce; pour over oysters. Top pie with remaining pastry; flute edges to seal. Cut slits in top crust for steam vents. Bake at 450 degrees for 30 minutes.

SHRIMP WITH ZIPPY COCKTAIL SAUCE

1/4 c. salt
1/4 c. vinegar
3 bay leaves
2 tsp. pickling spice
2 stalks celery and tops, chopped
4 lb. shrimp in shells

Combine salt, vinegar, bay leaves, pickling spice and celery in large kettle. Add 2 1/2 gallons water; bring to a boil. Add shrimp; cover. Reduce heat; simmer for 5 minutes. Rinse shrimp with cold water. Shell and devein shrimp; chill.

Zippy Cocktail Sauce

1 c. salad dressing or mayonnaise
1/4 c. catsup
3/4 c. chili sauce

2 1/2 tbsp. horseradish
3/4 tsp. salt
1 tbsp. vinegar

Combine all ingredients; blend until smooth. Chill. Yield: 12 servings.

Mrs. Annetta Balley
Agua Dulce, Texas

SALMON CROQUETTES

1 1-lb. can salmon
1/2 c. soft bread crumbs
1/4 tsp. grated onion
Dash of seasoned pepper
1 tsp. salt
1/2 can cream of mushroom soup
Cornmeal

Drain about half the liquid from salmon; flake salmon. Combine bread crumbs, onion, pepper, salt and soup; stir in salmon. Mix well. Chill for 2 hours. Shape salmon mixture into croquettes; roll in cornmeal. Fry in hot deep fat until browned.

Martha Rast
Henderson, Tennessee

CREAMED TUNA

1 7-oz. can tuna
1/2 c. sliced celery
2 tbsp. chopped onion
1 tbsp. butter or margarine
1 can Cheddar cheese soup
1/2 c. milk
2 tbsp. chopped pimento
1/2 c. green peas
Chopped parsley
Cooked rice

Drain and flake tuna. Cook celery and onion in butter in saucepan until tender. Blend in soup and milk. Add tuna, pimento and peas. Heat through, stirring occasionally. Garnish with parsley; serve over rice.

Ilona M. Wooten
Tyner, Tennessee

Casseroles

Casseroles are among the most wonderful and versatile dishes known to thrifty homemakers. They are a way to use leftovers . . . and introduce the family to sparkling new taste treats. They are quick and easy to prepare — with careful planning, you can always have a casserole in your freezer for that busy day's supper or when unexpected company drops in. Best of all, casseroles are low cost. They draw their flavor excitement from a blending of many flavors with just the right hint of seasoning — not from a lot of expensive ingredients.

With all these advantages, it's no wonder that some of the best recipes homemakers have developed are those for casseroles. In the pages that follow, you'll find economical recipes for delicious casseroles sure to bring compliments from family and guests.

These low-cost recipes are supplemented with household hints from thrifty-minded women — the precious bits of wisdom they use to keep their own food budgets in line.

Low-cost recipes for mouth-watering casseroles and hints to help you save even more — this casseroles section will become an invaluable part of your cooking library. Try it and see!

Casseroles

GETTING MORE FOR YOUR MONEY

Casseroles are one-dish main courses, vegetable courses, or desserts. They are much appreciated by today's busy homemaker because they usually can be prepared in advance and kept in the refrigerator or freezer until serving time. And casseroles are a wonderful way to use leftovers and create bright new flavor treats at the same time. In fact, for eye-appeal, economy, and hearty good flavor, it's hard to beat a casserole.

While American homemakers use the word "casserole" to describe a one-dish course, their French counterparts use the word to refer to a dish made especially for oven or top-of-the-stove cooking.

SEASONING YOUR CASSEROLES

A pinch of seasoning – herbs, spices, or vegetable – costs very little but adds a brand new world of flavor to your favorite casseroles. *Basil* goes well with tomato casseroles, those with a tomato sauce base, and with peas, string beans, potatoes, and spinach. *Chive* is a nice complement to casseroles made with beef, lamb, veal, and poultry. *Dill* is far stronger than either basil or chive and should be added toward the end of cooking. It is particularly nice with fish and beef casseroles. *Sweet marjoram* is a delicate herb that highlights the flavors of meat, fish, and seafood casseroles, as well as those made with peas, spinach, or green beans. *Rosemary* adds a mild flavor to game, lamb, pork, veal, and fish casseroles. Try it, too, in cauliflower, peas, or spinach dishes. *Thyme,* always used in combination with *bay leaf,* is good in casseroles of beans, potatoes, seafood, fish, beef, lamb, veal, and pork. *Oregano* is often used in combination with basil in tomato-based dishes. *Parsley* goes well with all meat dishes and is particularly nice mixed with butter crumbs for a casserole topping. *Sage* should be used sparingly and is good not just in stuffings but in dishes made with poultry, veal, or pork. *Mint* is a traditional herb in lamb dishes, but try it with peas, carrots, and snap beans – a new flavor treat awaits you!

Among the spices used with casseroles are *caraway,* in beet, potato, or cabbage casseroles; *cayenne,* in spicy-hot casseroles; *curry powder,* in poultry, seafood, and fish casseroles; and *paprika,* in casseroles made of fish, poultry, pork, or veal.

Onions are another low-cost way to bring new flavor excitement to your casseroles. A few *mushrooms* – low in price when you buy stems and pieces – will highlight almost every casserole. And don't forget *celery.* A real bargain at your produce counter, celery stalks and leaves add new flavor to tomato-based casseroles or those made with cauliflower, cheese, or game.

FREEZING YOUR CASSEROLES

One word of caution if you plan to freeze a casserole – don't use seasonings before freezing; wait until the dish is thawing. Freezing changes the flavor and texture of many seasonings.

Ingredients will react in different ways to freezing. Some are unchanged while others alter drastically. Eggs, for instance, should never be frozen unless they have been hard-cooked and sieved.

Some sauces and mayonnaise may separate during freezing but can be restored by stirring during the thawing process. Sauces which are egg-based should not be frozen, and those with milk and eggs tend to curdle.

Cheese does not freeze well – add sliced or grated cheese toppings after the casserole has thawed.

Potatoes should not be frozen, as they crumble and will cause your casserole to become mushy.

Noodles, spaghetti, and macaroni all have a far better flavor if they are added to casseroles during the thawing process.

Meats which have been frozen may be thawed, cooked in a casserole, and then refrozen without danger of contamination. However, very small pieces of meat may dry out if they are frozen.

Casseroles intended for the freezer should be only partially cooked. The pan is then plunged into ice water, chilled quickly, and wrapped for freezing.

Here's a hint that helps you cut down on the number of casserole dishes you use. When you are preparing a casserole to freeze, line the dish with heavy-duty foil, fill it with your casserole recipe, and cook and freeze it as usual. After the ingredients are thoroughly frozen, remove the foil from the dish, wrap the foil "dish" and its contents, and return to the freezer. Your casserole dish is ready to use again, and your delicious food stays safely frozen in its own foil package.

Wrapping makes the difference between success and failure in freezing. Moisture-proof, vapor-proof wrappings are a must. Try to get as much air as possible out of your freezer package – air left in packaged food draws on the moisture and juices of your casserole to form a frost. That frost gives off the odors of the casserole to other foods in your freezer.

Casseroles should be kept frozen at zero degrees or lower. When ready to thaw, pop them into an oven set at the temperature the recipe called for. (You will need more cooking time, however.) If your casserole is very large, it should be completely thawed in the refrigerator before being heated. Thawing large casseroles in the oven produces burnt edges and still-frozen centers.

MICROWAVE TACO CASSEROLE

1 lb. ground beef
1 15-oz. can tomato sauce
1 env. taco seasoning mix
1/4 c. chopped pimento-stuffed olives
1 6 1/2-oz. package corn chips, crushed
1 16-oz. can refried beans
1/2 c. shredded Cheddar cheese

Crumble ground beef into 1 1/2-quart glass dish. Microwave on High for 4 to 5 minutes or until no longer pink, stirring once; drain. Add tomato sauce, taco seasoning mix and olives; mix well. Microwave for 3 minutes or until boiling. Layer corn chips in pie plate. Spoon refried beans over chips, pressing down to form crust. Fill with ground beef mixture. Microwave for 3 minutes or until heated through. Top with cheese. Microwave for 1 minute. Serve with taco sauce or salsa.

Lillian M. Kwas
Gurnee, Illinois

TIMESAVING CASSEROLE IDEA

When preparing a casserole, double the amount of ingredients. Line 1 baking dish with foil and fill with casserole mixture. Freeze until firm. Remove the frozen block from the dish and wrap for storage, freeing the dish for use. Return the frozen block to the same dish to bake.

Carolyn W. Yeatts
Farmville, Virginia

HAMBURGER-MACARONI CASSEROLE

1 8-oz. package elbow macaroni
1 1/2 lb. ground beef
1/4 green pepper, chopped
1 med. onion, chopped
1 No. 303 can tomatoes
1 tbsp. catsup
1 tbsp. Worcestershire sauce
1 can mushroom soup
1 c. grated Cheddar cheese

Cook macaroni according to package directions; drain. Brown beef, green pepper and onion in 1 tablespoon fat in skillet; drain off fat. Add tomatoes, macaroni, catsup and Worcestershire sauce. Simmer for 30 minutes. Pour into large baking dish; add mushroom soup, stirring to mix well. Sprinkle cheese over top. Bake for 30 minutes at 350 degrees. Yield: 10-12 servings.

Mrs. Virginia Kendrick Craun
Barnsdall, Oklahoma

CHEESEBURGER CASSEROLE

1 lb. lean ground beef
1/4 c. chopped onion
3/4 tsp. salt
1/8 tsp. pepper
1/4 c. catsup
1 8-oz. can tomato sauce
8 oz. cheese
1 can biscuits or sesame seed rolls

Combine 2 tablespoons fat, beef and onion in skillet; cook until beef is lightly browned. Drain; add salt and pepper. Stir in catsup and tomato sauce; heat thoroughly. Turn into 8-inch square pan. Cut cheese into thin strips; spread over beef mixture. Top with biscuits. Bake at 425 degrees for 20 to 25 minutes or until biscuits are golden brown. Tomato soup may be substituted for tomato sauce if desired. Yield: 4-6 servings.

Myrtis L. McAlhany
Saint George, South Carolina

RAINY DAY BEEF DISH

1/4 lb. bacon, diced
1 1/2 lb. ground beef
2 lge. onions, chopped
2 green peppers, chopped
1 sm. can chopped mushrooms
1 can kidney beans
2 c. noodles, cooked
1 No. 2 can tomatoes
Grated cheese

Fry bacon in large ovenproof skillet until crisp. Add ground beef; cook, stirring, until beef is browned. Add onions, green peppers, mushrooms, kidney beans, noodles and tomatoes; mix well. Simmer for 1 hour. Sprinkle with cheese. Bake at 325 degrees until cheese is melted. Yield: 8 servings.

Mrs. Sara Yowell
Hayetteville, Arkansas

AMERICAN CHOP SUEY

1 lb. hamburger
3 stalks celery, minced
1 med. onion, minced
1 can cream of mushroom soup
1 can chicken soup
1 can celery soup
1 sm. box instant rice

Brown hamburger, celery and onion in skillet. Add soups and rice; mix thoroughly. Bake for 20 to 30 minutes at 375 degrees.

Mrs. Nancy Jones
Arlington, Texas

MICROWAVE STROGANOFF CASSEROLE

1 lb. ground beef, crumbled
1/4 c. chopped onion
2 cloves of garlic, minced
4 oz. medium noodles
1 c. sliced mushrooms
1 13-oz. can beef broth
Pepper to taste
8 oz. sour cream
2 tbsp. chopped parsley

Combine ground beef, onion and garlic in glass dish. Microwave on High for 5 minutes, stirring once; drain. Stir in noodles, mushrooms, broth and pepper. Microwave, covered, on Medium for 22 minutes, stirring once. Let stand for 2 minutes. Fold in sour cream. Sprinkle with parsley.

Melanie Potanin
Clayton, California

LASAGNA CASSEROLE

1 med. onion, chopped
2 cloves of garlic, chopped
1/4 c. olive oil
1 lb. ground beef, crumbled
1 No. 303 can tomato sauce
1 sm. can tomato paste
2 c. water
1/4 tsp. cayenne pepper
2 bay leaves
Dash of basil
Salt and pepper to taste
8 oz. lasagna, cooked
1 sm. carton cottage cheese
8 oz. mozzarella cheese
Grated Parmesan cheese

Saute onion and garlic in oil in skillet until golden brown. Add beef; saute until browned. Add tomato sauce, tomato paste, water, cayenne pepper, bay leaves, basil, salt and pepper; mix well. Simmer for 1 hour and 30 minutes. Arrange layers of lasagna, beef sauce, cottage cheese and mozzarella cheese in greased casserole, having 3 layers of each. Top with Parmesan cheese. Bake, uncovered, in 350-degree oven for 45 minutes.

Mrs. Jerry Knox
Metairie, Louisiana

DIET-WISE MICROWAVE SHORTCUT

For ground beef that is as fat-free as possible, crumble it into a colander set over a glass dish and microwave it until it is no longer pink. The fat will drip through the colander into the bowl and the ground beef is ready to use in all your favorite recipes.

Maggie Hart
Charleston, Tennessee

CORNED BEEF HASH CASSEROLE

8 oz. noodles
2 onions, chopped
3/4 green pepper, chopped
1 tbsp. butter
1 can cream of mushroom soup
1 c. milk
3/4 c. grated Velveeta cheese
1 can corned beef hash
3/4 c. buttered bread crumbs

Cook noodles according to package directions; drain. Place noodles in casserole. Saute onions and green pepper in butter in skillet. Add soup, milk and cheese. Cook, stirring, until cheese is melted. Add corned beef hash. Stir soup mixture into cooked noodles. Top with buttered bread crumbs. Bake at 350 degrees for about 30 minutes. Yield: 6-8 servings.

Mrs. Hank E. Zabor
Leesburg, Florida

VEAL SCALLOPINI AND RISOTTO

1 lb. veal
1 c. flour
Salt
Pepper to taste
Butter
1/2 c. sherry or red wine
1 3-oz. can mushrooms, drained
1/2 c. chopped onion
1 c. long grain rice
1 can beef consomme
Grated Parmesan cheese

Cut veal into 1-inch cubes. Combine flour, salt to taste and pepper. Coat veal with seasoned flour. Brown veal in hot butter in skillet; add sherry and mushrooms. Simmer for 10 minutes. Place in heated serving dish. Saute onion in 1/4 cup butter; stir in rice and brown lightly. Add enough water to consomme to make 2 cups liquid; pour into saucepan. Add 1/4 teaspoon salt; heat to boiling point. Stir in rice mixture; cover and simmer for 20 minutes. Stir in 1/4 cup butter; sprinkle with cheese. Serve over veal. Yield: 6-8 servings.

Mrs. Lavonne Schuetz
Arvin, California

CALIFORNIA VEAL CASSEROLE

2 1/3 c. sifted flour
4 tsp. baking powder
1/2 tsp. salt
1 tsp. poultry seasoning
1 tsp. celery seed
1 tsp. dry onion flakes
1/4 c. salad oil
1 c. milk
1/4 c. melted butter
1 c. bread crumbs
1 tsp. paprika
2 lb. veal round steak
1/4 c. shortening
1 1-lb. can sm. cooked onions
2 cans cream of chicken soup
1 soup can onion liquid
1 c. sour cream

Sift 2 cups flour, baking powder, salt and poultry seasoning together into bowl. Add celery seed and onion flakes. Blend in oil and milk, stirring until just moistened. Combine butter and bread crumbs; drop dough by rounded tablespoons into bread crumb mixture, rolling to coat. Mix remaining flour and paprika; pound into veal. Cut veal into 2-inch cubes; brown in shortening in skillet. Place veal in 3-quart casserole. Drain onions; add to veal. Heat 1 can soup in skillet; blend in onion liquid. Bring to a boil; pour over veal mixture. Bake at 350 degrees for 45 minutes or until tender. Top with dumplings. Increase oven temperature to 425 degrees; bake for 20 to 25 minutes longer or until browned. Heat remaining soup and sour cream to boiling point; serve sauce with veal casserole. Yield: 8 servings.

Mary Denton Pierce
Albany, Kentucky

STORING ONIONS

Onions placed in a jar with a tight-fitting lid and kept in the refrigerator will stay fresh. Use the same jar over and over. Onions stored in this manner will not cause odors in refrigerator.

Mrs. Sondra Gordon
Corning, Arkansas

PORK CHOP SCALLOP

6 pork chops
5 tbsp. butter
4 med. potatoes
1 sm. onion, chopped
2 tbsp. flour
1 tsp. salt
1/4 tsp. pepper
2 c. milk
1 tsp. soy sauce
1/2 c. sliced water chestnuts

Cook chops in 3 tablespoons butter in skillet for 15 minutes; drain. Pare and slice potatoes; cook in boiling salted water for 5 minutes. Drain. Cook onion in remaining butter until tender. Blend in flour, salt and pepper. Stir in milk and soy sauce gradually; cook until smooth and thickened, stirring constantly. Alternate layers of potatoes and water chestnuts in greased 2-quart casserole. Pour white sauce over all. Place pork chops on top; cover. Bake at 350 degrees for 25 to 30 minutes. Yield: 6 servings.

Mrs. Eleanor Hatch
Joseph, Oregon

MEADOW PORK CASSEROLE

6 pork chops
1 tsp. salt
Pepper to taste
Flour
2 tbsp. chopped onion
Chopped green pepper to taste
1 c. rice
1 No. 2 can stewed tomatoes

Season chops with salt and pepper; coat with flour. Cook chops, onion and green pepper in 3 tablespoons fat in skillet. Place rice in greased casserole; top with tomatoes. Arrange chops, onion and green pepper over tomatoes. Bake, covered, at 350 degrees for about 1 hour or until rice is tender.

Patty Maxwell
Gadsden, Alabama

CHOW MEIN CASSEROLE

1 lb. cubed pork
1/2 lb. round steak, cubed
1 1/2 c. diced onion
1 1/2 tsp. salt
1/2 tsp. pepper
1 1/2 c. sliced celery
1 1/2 c. bean sprouts
6 peeled radishes, sliced
1/2 c. cold water
4 tbsp. cornstarch
1 tbsp. soy sauce
1 1/2 tsp. sugar

Brown meats; add onion. Cook until transparent. Add salt, pepper, celery and 1 1/2 cups hot water. Cook for 10 minutes. Add bean sprouts and radishes. Pour meat mixture into casserole. Mix remaining ingredients. Pour cornstarch mixture over meat mixture. Bake at 350 degrees for 10 minutes. Serve hot over chow mein noodles if desired. Yield: 6 servings.

LeNora Hudson
Sulphur, Oklahoma

FREEZER PACKAGING HINT

Place pork chops to be frozen into individual used pint-sized plastic bags. Place small bags into larger bag; seal and freeze. Small bags are easily separated to reduce thawing time. Small bags may be used several times.

Mrs. Dorothy B. Byrd
Snellville, Georgia

FRENCH-FRIED POTATO-ALMOND SCALLOP

1 lb. lean boneless pork, cubed
3/4 lb. boneless veal, cubed
2 tbsp. butter or margarine
1 tsp. salt
1 10 1/2-oz. can cream of mushroom soup
1 10 1/2-oz. can cream of chicken soup
1 1-lb. package frozen French-fried potatoes
1/2 c. milk
1/2 c. sliced almonds
1/3 c. fine cereal crumbs

Brown pork and veal in butter in skillet over low heat, turning to brown evenly on all sides. Add 1/4 cup water and salt; cover skillet. Simmer for 1 hour and 30 minutes to 2 hours or until meats are tender. Add soups, French-fried potatoes, milk and 1/4 cup almonds; mix well. Spoon into shallow 2-quart casserole; sprinkle with cereal crumbs and remaining almonds. Bake in 350-degree oven for 30 to 40 minutes or until heated through. Yield: 6 servings.

HAM AND WALNUTS HAWAIIAN

1 13-oz. can pineapple tidbits
1 1/2 c. cooked ham cubes
2 c. cooked shell macaroni
1/2 c. sliced green seedless grapes
1 c. toasted walnut pieces
3 tbsp. butter
3 tbsp. all-purpose flour
1/2 tsp. salt
1/2 tsp. ground ginger
1 tsp. soy sauce
1/4 tsp. pepper
1 2/3 c. evaporated milk
3/4 c. chopped walnuts

Drain pineapple. Combine ham cubes, macaroni, pineapple, grapes and walnut pieces. Melt butter in skillet; stir in flour, salt, ginger, soy sauce and pepper. Stir in milk gradually. Cook until thickened, stirring constantly. Add sauce to walnut mixture; pour into 1 1/2-quart casserole. Bake at 350 degrees for about 20 minutes. Sprinkle chopped walnuts around edge of casserole; bake for 10 minutes longer.

BISCUIT-TOPPED HAM PIE

3 tbsp. chopped onion
1/4 c. chopped green pepper
6 tbsp. flour
1 can cream of chicken soup
1 1/3 c. milk
1 1/2 c. chopped boiled ham
1 tbsp. lemon juice
6 eggs, beaten
1 can refrigerator biscuits

Saute onion and green pepper in 4 tablespoons fat. Remove from heat; blend in flour until smooth. Add soup, milk and ham. Cook, stirring constantly, until thick; add lemon juice. Pour in baking dish. Stir eggs into ham mixture; place biscuits on top. Bake at 450 degrees for 15 minutes. Reduce heat to 375 degrees; bake for 15 minutes longer. Yield: 10 servings.

Mrs. Elodee McCormick
Dade City, Florida

HAM AND MACARONI CASSEROLE

1/2 lb. elbow macaroni
Butter
4 tsp. minced onion
1 tbsp. flour
1/4 tsp. dry mustard
1/2 tsp. salt
Dash of pepper
2 c. milk
1 1/2 c. slivered cooked ham
2 c. grated Cheddar cheese
3/4 c. fresh bread crumbs

Cook macaroni according to package directions; drain. Melt 2 tablespoons butter in double boiler; add onion, flour, dry mustard, salt and pepper. Stir in milk gradually; cook until smooth and thickened, stirring constantly. Add ham and 1 1/2 cups cheese; cook, stirring until cheese is melted. Arrange macaroni in greased 2-quart casserole; pour on ham sauce. Toss lightly with fork until macaroni is coated. Sprinkle remaining cheese over top. Blend 4 teaspoons melted butter and bread crumbs together; sprinkle crumbs over cheese. Bake for 20 minutes at 400 degrees. Yield: 4-6 servings.

Mrs. Olga Banks
Midland, Texas

HAM AND EGG CASSEROLE

1 c. diced cooked ham
2 hard-cooked eggs, sliced
2 c. thick white sauce
Buttered bread crumbs

Layer ham and eggs in casserole; add half the white sauce. Repeat layers; top with bread crumbs. Bake at 400 degrees until golden brown. Yield: 6 servings.

Mrs. Ruth Phillips
Garrison, Texas

MICROWAVE CHICKEN WITH MUSHROOMS

1/2 c. butter
1/2 c. fine bread crumbs
3 tbsp. Parmesan cheese
1 tsp. each basil and oregano
1/2 tsp. each garlic salt and paprika
1/4 tsp. each salt and pepper
6 chicken breasts, skinned
1 med. onion, chopped
1 4-oz. can mushrooms, drained
1 tbsp. chopped parsley
1/4 c. dry white wine

Microwave butter on High in glass dish for 45 seconds or until melted. Combine bread crumbs, cheese and seasonings on waxed paper. Rinse chicken and pat dry. Dip into butter; roll in crumb mixture, coating well. Place in 7 x 11-inch glass dish. Microwave for 6 minutes per pound of chicken, turning chicken once. Let stand, covered with foil, for 10 minutes. Add onion to butter remaining in dish. Microwave on High for 1 minute. Add mushrooms. Microwave for 1 minute. Stir in parsley. Microwave wine in glass measure for 30 seconds. Stir into mushroom mixture. Spoon over chicken.

Nancy McBride
San Jose, California

CHICKEN-HAM CASSEROLE

4 chicken breasts
Salt to taste
4 slices cooked ham
1 can cream of mushroom soup
1/2 c. chicken broth
2 hard-cooked eggs, chopped
1 tbsp. chopped pimento
2 tbsp. butter
1 c. crushed cracker crumbs
Grated Parmesan cheese to taste

Simmer chicken in boiling salted water until tender. Arrange ham slices in casserole with chicken on each slice. Combine soup, broth, eggs and pimento; pour over meats. Combine butter, crumbs and cheese; sprinkle over meat mixture. Bake at 350 degrees for 15 to 18 minutes or until bubbly.

Doris S. Hamilton
Laurel, Mississippi

HUNTINGTON CHICKEN CASSEROLE

3 c. chicken broth
1 lge. green pepper, chopped
1 lge. onion, chopped
3 stalks celery, chopped
3 oz. noodles
1 2-oz. can sliced mushrooms
1 4-oz. can chopped pimentos
Cooked chicken, diced
Salt and pepper to taste
1 c. grated American cheese

Bring broth to a boil; add green pepper, onion and celery. Cook for 15 minutes or until onion is transparent. Add noodles; cook for 10 minutes. Add remaining ingredients, reserving 1/4 cup cheese. Mix well; pour into 2-quart casserole. Top with reserved cheese. Bake at 350 degrees for 15 minutes. Yield: 8-10 servings.

Ruth Wiman
Roscoe, Texas

QUICK CHICKEN CASSEROLE

1 6-oz. can boned chicken
1 can cream of chicken soup
1 c. diced celery
2 tsp. minced onion
1/2 c. chopped pecans
1/2 tsp. salt
1/4 tsp. pepper
1 tbsp. lemon juice
3/4 c. mayonnaise
3 hard-cooked eggs, thinly sliced
2 c. crushed potato chips

Drain and dice chicken, reserving broth. Combine chicken, broth, soup, celery, onion, pecans, salt, pepper, lemon juice, mayonnaise and eggs. Spoon into 1-quart baking dish; sprinkle with potato chips. Bake at 450 degrees for 15 minutes or until lightly brown. Yield: 6-8 servings.

Mrs. Helen S. Underwood
Shepherdsville, Kentucky

CHICKEN LIVERS BAKED WITH RICE

3/4 lb. chicken livers
Salt and pepper
Flour
4 tbsp. butter or margarine
3 tbsp. minced onion
3 tbsp. finely chopped celery
1 c. uncooked rice
2 c. chicken broth
1 tsp. minced parsley

Sprinkle chicken livers with salt and pepper; shake in small amount of flour in paper bag. Brown quickly in butter in hot skillet; place in 6-cup casserole. Saute onion, celery and rice in butter remaining in skillet until slightly browned. Add chicken broth; stir well. Add parsley; pour over chicken livers. Cover tightly. Bake at 350 degrees for 30 minutes or until rice is tender and has absorbed the liquid. Add salt, if needed.

Imogene Brashear
Palatka, Florida

TURKEY CASSEROLE SUPREME

3 c. chicken consomme
1/3 c. rice
2 1/2 c. diced cooked turkey
3/4 c. chopped celery
1/4 c. chopped pimento
2 eggs, beaten
Salt
Dash of poultry seasoning
2 tbsp. onion, minced
3 tbsp. butter
3 tbsp. flour
1/2 c. heavy cream
1 c. sliced mushrooms
Pepper

Bring 2 cups consomme to a boil in saucepan; add rice. Cover; reduce heat. Simmer for 10 minutes. Stir in turkey, celery, pimento, eggs, 3/4 teaspoon salt and poultry seasoning; mix well. Pour into greased casserole. Bake at 325 degrees for 45 minutes. Saute onion lightly in butter; blend in flour. Add remaining consomme and cream slowly; cook over low heat until thickened, stirring constantly. Add mushrooms; season to taste with salt and pepper. Heat through and serve over turkey casserole.

Thelma S. Vogel
McAlester, Oklahoma

CRUSTY TURKEY CASSEROLE

2 c. fine noodles
1 env. dry cream of mushroom soup mix
1 c. milk
1 c. chopped cooked turkey
1/8 tsp. curry powder
1/4 tsp. pepper
1/4 tsp. hot sauce
1/2 tsp. salt
2 tbsp. salad oil
2 cloves of garlic, sliced
1 c. packaged bread crumbs
1/4 c. chopped parsley

Cook noodles according to package directions; drain well. Combine soup mix and 2 cups water in saucepan; bring to a boil. Remove from heat; let stand for about 10 minutes. Combine noodles, soup, milk, turkey and seasonings; mix well. Turn into casserole. Heat oil in skillet; add garlic. Saute garlic lightly. Remove garlic from oil; stir in bread crumbs and parsley. Spread over turkey mixture. Cover baking dish with foil; refrigerate overnight. Remove foil. Bake at 375 degrees for 30 minutes.

Mrs. Martha J. Barr
Fluvanna, Texas

SEAFOOD CASSEROLE

1 lb. fresh scallops
1 lb. crab meat
1 can cream of shrimp soup
1 c. sour cream
1/4 c. dry vermouth
1/2 tsp. dillweed
1 med. onion, chopped
2 tbsp. butter
2 c. bread crumbs
2 tbsp. melted butter
1/4 c. Parmesan cheese

Place scallops in glass dish. Microwave on High for 3 to 4 minutes or until cooked through. Combine with crab meat in 9-inch glass dish. Combine soup, sour cream, wine and dillweed in bowl; mix well. Pour over seafood. Combine onion and 2 tablespoons butter in dish. Microwave on High until transparent. Sprinkle over casserole. Mix bread crumbs and 2 tablespoons butter in bowl. Sprinkle over onions. Top with Parmesan cheese. Microwave on High until bubbly.

Vivian Gorodetsky
Ft. Myers, Florida

CHEESE IN MICROWAVE RECIPES

Cheese should always be added to microwave dishes as close as possible to the end of the cooking time, as it has a tendency to become rubbery. Process cheese and softer cheese work better in microwave recipes than hard natural cheeses. To top dishes with cheese, sprinkle it on during the standing time; the heat of the dish will melt it sufficiently.

Etta Cavener
Eureka Springs, Arkansas

SALMON-NOODLE CASSEROLE

1/4 c. butter
1/4 c. flour
1/4 tsp. dry mustard
1/4 tsp. paprika
1 tsp. salt
1 tall can evaporated milk
2 4-oz. cans sliced mushrooms
1 tsp. Worcestershire sauce
1 tbsp. lemon juice
1/4 c. grated Parmesan cheese
1 1-lb. can salmon
1/2 c. sliced stuffed olives
1 8-oz. package med. noodles
Buttered cheese cracker crumbs

Preheat oven to 375 degrees. Melt butter in medium saucepan; remove from heat. Blend in flour, mustard, paprika and salt; stir in milk. Drain mushrooms, reserving liquid. Add enough water to reserved liquid to measure 1 cup; add to butter mixture. Cook, stirring, over medium heat until thickened. Stir in Worcestershire sauce, lemon juice and cheese. Drain and flake salmon; fold salmon, olives and mushrooms into white sauce. Cook noodles according to package directions; drain. Add noodles to salmon mixture, blending well; spoon into lightly greased 2-quart casserole. Top with cheese cracker crumbs. Bake for 30 minutes.

TUNA AU GRATIN

Sifted flour
1/2 tsp. salt
1/2 c. shortening
4 to 5 tbsp. cold water
1 can mushroom soup
1/4 c. milk
2 tbsp. onion flakes
1 pkg. frozen peas, thawed
2 cans tuna, drained
1 4-oz. can pimento, chopped
1 c. grated cheese

Sift 1 1/2 cups flour and salt together; cut in shortening. Add cold water, stirring in quickly to form dough. Roll out 2/3 of the dough on floured surface. Line pastry pan with dough; flute edge and prick with fork. Roll out remaining dough; place on baking sheet. Bake pastry shell and dough on baking sheet at 450 degrees for 12 minutes or until lightly browned. Crumble dough on baking sheet for topping. Combine soup, milk, 2 tablespoons flour and onion flakes in saucepan. Cook over low heat, stirring constantly, until thickened. Remove from heat; stir in peas, tuna and pimento. Spoon filling into baked pie shell; top with pastry crumbs and cheese. Bake at 425 degrees for 12 to 15 minutes or until cheese melts. Yield: 6 servings.

Mrs. Hazel R. Dees
Paris, Texas

TUNA CASSEROLE

1/2 pkg. noodles
1 green pepper, minced
1/2 c. water
1 c. milk
1 can cream of mushroom soup
1 7-oz. can tuna, drained
2 hard-cooked eggs, chopped
1/2 c. buttered bread crumbs

Cook noodles according to package directions; drain. Combine green pepper and water in saucepan; heat slowly for 5 minutes. Combine milk and soup; add tuna, eggs and green pepper mixture. Alternate layers of noodles and tuna mixture in casserole. Top with buttered crumbs. Bake at 400 degrees for 30 minutes. Yield: 6-8 servings.

C. L. Owen
Madison, Tennessee

DEVILED EGGS IN TOMATO SAUCE

6 deviled eggs
1/4 c. minced onion
1/2 c. diced celery
1/2 stick margarine
3 tbsp. flour
1 can tomato soup
1/2 soup can water
Seasoning to taste

Place eggs in casserole. Saute onion and celery in margarine until golden brown; remove celery and onion from pan. Blend flour into pan drippings; add soup and water, stirring constantly. Cook until thickened; add onion, celery and seasoning. Pour soup mixture over eggs. Bake at 350 degrees for 20 minutes. Serve over rice. Yield: 6 servings.

Sister M. John Vianney
Gary, Indiana

EGG AND CHEESE CASSEROLE

1 c. shredded sharp Cheddar cheese
1 1/2 c. med. white sauce
1 1/2 c. buttered bread crumbs
4 hard-cooked eggs, sliced

Add cheese to white sauce in saucepan. Cook over low heat until cheese melts. Arrange layers of crumbs, cheese sauce and eggs in greased 1 1/2-quart baking dish. Bake at 400 degrees for 15 to 20 minutes or until brown. Serve hot. Yield: 4 servings.

Mrs. Mary Jane McNary
Daleville, Indiana

Vegetables & Side Dishes

To add bright notes of color and flavor . . . to highlight your main course . . . to balance your family's nutritional intake . . . of course you depend upon vegetables and accompaniments.

Homemakers know that yellow and green vegetables are invaluable sources of the vitamins and minerals all of us need every day. And they like fruit, pickles, sauces, and other accompaniments for the same reason. Best of all, these eye-pleasing additions to your dining table are some of the best bargains your supermarket offers.

Such appreciation of vegetables and other accompaniments is reflected in this section. From the kitchens of America's thriftiest homemakers come delightful recipes for tasty vegetables and sure-to-please accompaniments for every meal. With these wonderful recipes, you'll find a treasure trove of hints these great cooks pass on to you – to help you get more for your food dollar.

You'll enjoy browsing through these pages . . . and picturing brightly colored vegetables and accompaniments adding festive notes to your every meal. And your family is sure to take delighted pleasure in all the delicious, low-cost dishes you'll prepare!

Vegetables & Side Dishes

GETTING MORE FOR YOUR MONEY

FRESH VEGETABLES

Some supermarkets will have excellent produce, but others only mediocre. Your better buys can probably be found at local produce or farmers' markets. Another good source is the country roadside stand. And if you have an ethnic community in your town, check their produce markets – the variety is apt to be wider and the prices lower.

Your very best buys are when produce is at the peak of its season. Here are a few of the more popular vegetables and when they are in season.

Artichokes	April and May
Asparagus	Mid-February
Beans	Year-round
Beets	Year-round
Broccoli	Year-round, but scarcer in July and August
Brussels Sprouts	Best in October through December, but available year-round
Cabbage	Year-round
Carrots	Year-round
Cauliflower	September to January
Corn	May through September
Eggplant	Year-round, but best in late summer
Mushrooms	Peak in fall and winter
Parsnips	Year-round, but flavor is best in late winter
Peppers	Late summer
Potatoes	Year-round
Rutabagas	Fall and winter
Squash	Summer varieties in summer months; other varieties in fall and winter
Sweet Potatoes	Year-round
Turnips	Year-round

FROZEN VEGETABLES

Among the vegetables which are good when frozen are tiny green peas, corn, and mushrooms. During the off-season, frozen vegetables may be an excellent buy for you, especially if there is a discount for shopping in quantity.

Beware of limp or damp packages – these are telltale signs that the packages have been defrosted at least once. If frozen vegetables should defrost, use them as quickly as possible. Both nutrients and flavor are lost when vegetables are thawed and refrozen, then thawed, cooked, and served.

CANNED VEGETABLES

Private labels are usually packed by the top-grade canners but are priced well below those canners' lines. The only way to be sure of what you are getting in a store brand is to try one or two cans and see.

Some canned produce may be inspected and graded by a U. S. Department of Agriculture inspector. The most frequently found grades are "A," extra fancy (the kind you would use for a special occasion); "B," suitable for use alone or in casseroles or gelatin salads; and "C," inexpensive and just right for souffles, soups, or purees.

WHICH IS THE BEST BUY?

The only way to tell which among fresh, frozen, or canned vegetables is the best buy is to compare the cost per serving. It generally takes between one-third and one-half of a pound of fresh vegetables for one serving – or one to two ears of corn.

Canned vegetables come in different sized containers. An eight-ounce can serves two; sixteen-ounce cans and number 303 cans serve three to four. Number two cans serve four to five, number two and a half serve six to seven, and the number three cans serve eight to twelve.

Frozen vegetables usually come in packages ranging from ten ounces to sixteen ounces. The average package of frozen vegetables serves three to four people.

ACCOMPANIMENTS

Next time you have dry bread, try this budget-saving way to make your own *croutons.* Cut leftover bread into small cubes. Put them in a bag and shake in some garlic salt or another of your family's favorite seasonings. Shake the bag gently to mix the seasoning with the cubes. Then, the next time you have turned off your oven after baking, place a cookie sheet with a single layer of these bread cubes into the oven and let it sit until the oven has cooled. These croutons can be stored for a long time in a tightly sealed jar or can.

Marinated artichokes cost over a dollar for eight ounces. Yet in the vegetable section, you can purchase artichokes packed in water for less than half the price of the gourmet fare. Make your own spiced oil and let the artichokes marinate for at least twelve hours. And don't forget to save the oil – you can use it over and over.

Consider, too, the expensively priced can of *pickled beets.* If you buy beets in water and marinate them in your own mixture of vinegar, water, salt, and spices, you'll have a delicious accompaniment, for very little money.

ASPARAGUS AND ALMOND SAUCE

1 10-oz. package frozen asparagus
1/2 c. slivered blanched almonds
3/8 c. butter
3 tbsp. flour
1 c. milk
1 c. light cream
3/4 tsp. salt
Dash of pepper
2 c. instant rice

Cook asparagus according to package directions; drain. Saute almonds in 1/4 cup butter in saucepan until browned, stirring constantly. Remove almonds from pan. Blend flour into pan drippings; add milk gradually, stirring constantly. Add cream, salt and pepper. Cook over low heat until sauce is thickened, stirring constantly. Add asparagus and almonds. Prepare rice according to package directions. Add remaining butter; toss lightly. Pour sauce over rice to serve.

Pamela Kay Mowrey
Mechanicsburg, Pennsylvania

ASPARAGUS AND ONIONS

1 1-lb. can English peas, drained
1 14-oz. can asparagus, drained
1 14-oz. can sm. onions, drained, sliced
1 can cream of mushroom soup
1 c. grated American cheese

Layer peas, asparagus, onions and soup in casserole. Top with grated cheese. Cover with foil. Bake at 400 degrees for 40 minutes. Serve hot. Yield: 8 servings.

Mrs. Dorothy B. Byrd
Snellville, Georgia

BEANS AMANDINE

1 can mushroom soup
2 tbsp. flour
3 tbsp. butter, melted
3/4 c. shredded cheese
1/4 c. slivered almonds
1 lge. can French-style green beans, drained
3/4 c. buttered bread crumbs (opt.)

Combine soup and flour in bowl. Add butter, cheese, almonds and beans; mix well. Pour into casserole. Bake at 375 degrees for 30 to 40 minutes or until bubbly. Top with buttered bread crumbs. Bake until light brown. Yield: 6-8 servings.

Mrs. Elizabeth C. Wilson
Greensboro, Alabama

GREEN BEAN CASSEROLE

2 cans French-style green beans
1 c. water chestnuts, thinly sliced
1 c. bean sprouts, drained
1 med. onion, chopped
1 can mushroom soup
1/3 c. water
Salt to taste
1/2 c. cheese, grated
1 can French-fried onion rings

Place half the beans in 2-quart casserole; cover with half the water chestnuts, bean sprouts, and onion. Cover with half the soup diluted with the 1/3 cup water. Sprinkle with salt and cheese. Repeat layers. Bake at 400 degrees for 20 to 30 minutes. Reduce heat to 300 degrees. Top casserole with onion rings. Bake for 10 minutes longer.

Mrs. Rebecca McGaughy
Montevallo, Alabama

DOUBLE DUTY FOR DOUBLE BOILER COOKING

Cook vegetables in bottom of double boiler while preparing cheese sauce or other recipe in top of double boiler. This saves both time and fuel.

Mrs. Donna Brown
Wolfe City, Texas

MARINATED GREEN BEANS

1/2 c. cider vinegar
1/4 c. cold water
1 1/2 tbsp. cooking oil
1/4 tsp. salt
1/4 tsp. pepper
1/2 c. sugar
1 No. 303 can whole green beans
1 med. onion, thinly sliced

Blend vinegar, water, oil, salt, pepper and sugar together for marinade. Arrange alternate layers of beans and onion in dish; cover with marinade. Cover; refrigerate overnight. Serve cold. Yield: 6-8 servings.

Jane T. Nix
Atlanta, Georgia

FULL OF BEANS CASSEROLE

1 pkg. frozen green limas, cooked
1 pkg. frozen French-style green beans, cooked
1 pkg. frozen green peas, cooked
1 can condensed cheese soup
1/2 c. half and half
1 c. corn flake crumbs
3 tbsp. melted butter
1 tbsp. parsley, finely chopped

Mix beans and peas in greased casserole. Combine soup and milk in bowl. Pour over vegetables. Blend corn flake crumbs and butter; sprinkle over cheese sauce. Sprinkle parsley on top. Bake at 300 degrees for 30 minutes. Yield: 8-10 servings.

Minta A. Palmer
Buda, Texas

BAKED BEAN POT

2 c. dry navy beans
1 1/2 qt. cold water
1 1/2 tsp. salt
1 sm. onion, sliced
4 tbsp. butter or margarine
1/4 c. catsup
1/4 c. molasses
1 tsp. dry mustard

Rinse beans; place in cold water in saucepan. Bring to boiling point; cook for 2 minutes. Remove from heat; cover. Let stand for 1 hour. Add 1 teaspoon salt; simmer, covered, for 1 hour or until beans are tender. Drain; reserve stock. Place onion in 2-quart bean pot or casserole; add beans. Combine 2 1/4 cups bean stock with butter, catsup, molasses, dry mustard and remaining salt; pour over beans. Bake, covered, at 325 degrees for 4 hours. Add bean stock or water as needed. Uncover; bake for 30 minutes longer or until brown. Yield: 6 servings.

Mrs. Dorothy H. Lee
Allen, Oklahoma

BABY LIMA BEANS

1 can condensed mushroom soup
1 pkg. frozen baby green lima beans, thawed
1 tbsp. finely chopped onion
1 tbsp. Worcestershire sauce
Salt and pepper to taste
Buttered crumbs

Bring soup and beans to a boil in saucepan. Add onion, Worcestershire sauce and seasonings. Pour into baking dish; top with crumbs. Bake at 350 degrees for 20 to 25 minutes.

Agnes D. Ingram
Mount Gilead, North Carolina

SAVING BURNED BEANS

Remove beans from scorched pan; place in another saucepan. Add a small amount of liquid. Place a slice of bread or toast on top of beans to absorb the burned taste. Resume cooking as usual.

Dorothy Rousseaw
Baton Rouge, Louisiana

BROCCOLI PARMESAN FOR A CROWD

4 boxes frozen broccoli
3 tbsp. minced onion
3 tbsp. margarine
3 tbsp. flour
3/4 tsp. salt
Dash of pepper
1/2 tsp. dry mustard
1/8 tsp. marjoram
1 1/2 c. milk
1 can cream of chicken soup
3/4 c. grated Parmesan cheese
Paprika to taste
1 can French-fried onion rings

Cook broccoli in small amount of water for 5 minutes or just until bright green and thawed; drain. Arrange in shallow 12 x 7 1/2-inch baking dish. Saute onion in margarine until tender; blend in flour, salt, pepper, mustard and marjoram. Add milk and soup; cook, stirring constantly, until thickened. Add 1/2 cup Parmesan cheese; stir until melted. Pour sauce over broccoli. Sprinkle with paprika and remaining cheese. Scatter onion rings over top. Bake at 375 degrees for 25 minutes. Yield: 10-12 servings.

Mrs. Ina Mae Perry
Lexington, Texas

MICROWAVE BROCCOLI CASSEROLE

2 10-oz. packages frozen chopped broccoli
1 onion, chopped
1/4 c. margarine
1/2 c. milk
1 c. minute rice
1 8-oz. jar Cheez Whiz
1 can cream of mushroom soup

Microwave broccoli using package directions; drain. Combine onion and margarine in glass dish. Microwave on High for 2 minutes. Stir in broccoli, milk, rice, Cheez Whiz, soup and 1/4 cup water; mix well. Microwave on High for 15 minutes. Yield: 6 servings.

Linda Kaufmann
Crescent City, California

FRESH VEGETABLE SKILLET STEW

4 c. fresh broccoli
2 tbsp. salad oil
1 clove of garlic, minced
1 lb. lean pork, cut into 1/4-in. strips
2 peeled carrots, cut into 1/4-in. strips
1 med. onion, cut into 1/4-in. strips
1/4 c. soy sauce
2 tbsp. Sherry
1 tbsp. cornstarch
2 tsp. sugar
1/8 tsp. each ginger, salt

Cut broccoli stalks into 1/8-inch thick rounds. Break head of broccoli into small flowerettes. Heat salad oil and garlic in 10-inch skillet. Add pork and broccoli stem pieces. Cook over high heat for 5 minutes or until pork is no longer pink, stirring constantly. Add broccoli flowerettes, carrots and onion strips. Reduce heat. Cook, covered, for 5 minutes or until tender-crisp, stirring occasionally. Mix remaining ingredients; pour into skillet. Bring to a boil. Reduce heat; simmer for 2 minutes or until sauce is thickened. Yield: 4 servings.

Shirley Edmondson
Montgomery, Alabama

SWEET AND SOUR RED CABBAGE

4 tbsp. shortening
1 med. red cabbage, shredded
2 apples, chopped
1/2 tsp. salt
1/4 c. sugar
1/2 tsp. caraway seed
Chopped onion to taste
1/4 c. cider vinegar

Melt shortening in saucepan or in electric frying pan; add cabbage. Fry cabbage, turning occasionally, until edges are browned; add apples, seasonings, onion and vinegar. Cover; cook for 15 minutes.

Mrs. Louise Sturgeon
Detroit, Michigan

MICROWAVE GLAZED CARROTS AND RAISINS

2 c. 1 1/2-inch julienne carrots
2 tbsp. raisins
1 tbsp. butter
1 tbsp. brown sugar
1/2 tsp. grated lemon rind
1/8 tsp. salt

Combine carrots and 1 tablespoon water in 1-quart glass dish. Microwave, covered, on High for 4 1/2 to 5 1/2 minutes or until tender-crisp, stirring once; drain. Add raisins, butter, brown sugar, lemon rind and salt; mix lightly. Microwave, covered, for 1 minute or until butter is melted. Mix to coat carrots evenly. Yield: 4 servings.

Cindy Harmon
Savannah, Georgia

MICROWAVE VEGETABLE SHORTCUT

You can cook vegetables to use in a casserole right in the package. Remove outer wrappings and pierce the package with a fork. Microwave using the package directions. Let stand for several minutes; squeeze gently to remove excess moisture. Use as directed in your recipe.

Mary Lou Wilson
La Mesa, New Mexico

ZESTY LOW-COST CARROTS

6 to 8 carrots, cut lengthwise
2 tbsp. grated onion
2 tbsp. horseradish
1/2 c. mayonnaise
1/2 tsp. salt
1/4 tsp. pepper
1/4 c. cracker crumbs
1 tbsp. butter, melted
Dash of paprika

Cook carrots in water to cover until tender; drain. Place in shallow baking dish. Combine 1/4 cup water, onion, horseradish, mayonnaise, salt and pepper; pour over carrots. Combine cracker crumbs, butter and paprika; toss to mix. Spread over carrot mixture. Bake at 375 degrees for 15 to 20 minutes. Yield: 6 servings.

Naomi Austin
Gainesville, Texas

CELERY SAVINGS

Wash and chop small celery stems and tops that are ordinarily discarded. Store in plastic containers in freezer for use in soups and casseroles.

Mrs. Dorthy G. Wood
Staunton, Virginia

FRENCH-BRAISED CELERY

2 c. 1-in. pieces of celery
4 sprigs of parsley
4 slices onion
1/2 c. bouillon
1 tsp. salt
1/4 tsp. pepper
2 strips bacon, diced
Buttered bread crumbs

Place celery, parsley, onion slices and bouillon in casserole; sprinkle with salt, pepper and bacon. Cover. Bake at 375 degrees for 30 minutes. Sprinkle with buttered bread crumbs; bake, uncovered, for 10 minutes longer or until crumbs are browned.

Mary Ann Hribek
Giddings, Texas

SCALLOPED CELERY

3 c. sliced celery
1 c. chopped green peppers
Chopped onion to taste
1/2 can cream of celery soup
Salt and pepper to taste
Cracker crumbs

Cook celery, green peppers and onion in small amount water until tender. Drain. Add soup and seasonings. Place in greased 1-quart casserole. Top with cracker crumbs. Bake at 350 degrees until heated through.

Mrs. Jane Erickson Peterson
Minneapolis, Minnesota

NO-WASTE CORN ON THE COB

Blanch corn on the cob then cool in ice water. Wrap each ear separately in aluminum foil, making sure the ends are well covered. Store in home freezer. Remove the exact number of ears needed. Drop wrapped corn into pot of boiling water; return to a boil. Cook for about 8 to 10 minutes. Serve in foil.

Rachel Brewster
Pottsboro, Texas

MICROWAVE SOUTHERN CREAMED CORN

10 ears fresh corn
6 tbsp. butter
1 tbsp. flour
1/2 tsp. salt
1/4 c. (or more) milk

Cut kernels from corn ears; scrape cobs. Microwave butter on High in 1-quart glass dish for 30 seconds or until melted. Blend in flour and salt. Add corn and milk; mix well. Microwave, covered, on High for 4 minutes. Stir corn and turn dish. Microwave, covered, for 6 minutes longer or until tender, adding additional milk 1 tablespoon at a time if necessary to make of desired consistency. Let stand for 3 minutes.

Darla Blitz
Columbus, Mississippi

MICROWAVE SHOE PEG CORN CASSEROLE

1/2 c. onion
1 c. chopped celery
1/2 c. shredded Cheddar cheese
1 16-oz. can whole kernel corn, drained
1 16-oz. can French-style green beans, drained
1/2 c. chopped green bell pepper
1 can cream of celery soup
1 cup sour cream
1/2 c. melted margarine
1 stack round butter crackers, crushed

Combine onion, celery, cheese, corn, green beans, green pepper, soup and sour cream in bowl; mix well. Spoon into greased shallow glass dish. Combine margarine and cracker crumbs in bowl; mix well. Sprinkle over casserole. Microwave on High for 10 to 15 minutes or until bubbly. Yield: 6 servings.

Elaine Vollmer
New Braunfels, Texas

EGGPLANT PARMIGIANA

1 lge. eggplant
Salt

4 tbsp. butter
1 lb. ground beef
Margarine
2 tbsp. chopped parsley
1/2 c. chopped onion
1/4 tsp. pepper
4 peeled tomatoes, sliced
1/4 c. grated Parmesan cheese
3 slices mozzarella cheese

Cut eggplant into 12 slices; sprinkle with salt. Let stand for 5 minutes; pat dry. Saute in butter until golden brown; drain on paper towel. Brown beef in small amount margarine; stir in parsley, onion, pepper, 1 teaspoon salt and tomatoes. Cook for about 10 minutes. Place 6 eggplant slices in shallow casserole; add beef sauce. Top with remaining eggplant; cover with Parmesan cheese and mozzarella cheese. Bake at 350 degrees for 30 minutes. Yield: 6 servings.

Linda Louise Givens
Richmond, Virginia

RICE-STUFFED EGGPLANT

2/3 c. chopped green peppers
2/3 c. chopped celery
1 c. chopped onions
2 tbsp. butter
1/2 c. uncooked rice
1 lge. eggplant
1 1-lb. 13-oz. can tomatoes
1 1/2 tsp. salt
1/8 tsp. pepper
1 tsp. sweet basil
2 tsp. Worcestershire sauce
Grated cheese

Saute green peppers, celery and onions in butter; push vegetables to one side. Add rice; saute until golden brown, stirring occasionally. Halve eggplant; scoop out pulp, leaving 1/2-inch shell. Chop pulp; add to rice mixture. Stir in tomatoes and seasonings. Simmer, covered, for 20 minutes or until rice is tender; turn into eggplant shell. Bake at 350 degrees for 1 hour. Sprinkle with cheese. Yield: 5-6 servings.

Elceone Roberts
Alta Loma, Texas

SPANISH OKRA

1/4 lb. okra, cut 1/4 in. thick
2 lge. fresh tomatoes, diced
3 tbsp. chopped onion
1 tsp. salt
4 tbsp. butter
2 tbsp. chili powder
3 drops of Tabasco sauce
1 c. water

Saute okra, tomatoes, onion and salt in butter for 5 minutes. Add chili powder, Tabasco sauce and water; mix well. Simmer, covered, over low heat until vegetables are tender and mixture has thickened. Yield: 6-8 servings.

Mrs. Georgia Short
Dell City, Texas

ONION CASSEROLE

9 lge. onions, peeled
Salt and pepper to taste
1 slice bacon, diced
1 tbsp. chopped green pepper
1/2 c. chopped ham
Garlic to taste
1/2 c. tomato puree
1/2 c. grated cheese

Arrange onions in greased baking dish; sprinkle with salt and pepper. Add bacon, green pepper, ham, garlic and tomato puree. Cover. Bake at 350 degrees for 20 minutes. Remove cover; sprinkle with cheese. Bake for 20 to 30 minutes longer. Yield: 4-5 servings.

Mrs. Kate S. Berry
Latta, South Carolina

DEVILED PEAS

1 No. 2 can English peas, drained
1 sm. can pimento, chopped
1 green pepper, minced
1 c. grated cheese
1 tsp. Worcestershire sauce
1 sm. can mushrooms, drained
1 can cream of tomato soup
1 c. finely chopped celery
1/2 c. chili sauce
6 hard-cooked eggs, sliced
1 1/2 c. thick white sauce

Combine all ingredients except eggs and white sauce; mix well. Arrange layers of peas mixture, sauce and eggs in greased casserole. Garnish top with crumbs, butter and additional grated cheese if desired. Bake at 350 degrees for 20 to 30 minutes. One can cream of mushroom soup may replace white sauce.

Mrs. Doris Griffith
Eclectic, Alabama

MICROWAVE PARTY POTATOES

8 med. potatoes, peeled, chopped
8 oz. cream cheese, softened
8 oz. French onion dip
1 1/2 tsp. salt
1/2 tsp. garlic salt
Pepper to taste
Butter
1/2 tsp. paprika

Combine potatoes with 1/2 cup water in 3-quart glass dish. Microwave, covered, on High for 10 minutes or until potatoes are tender; drain. Beat cream cheese, onion dip, salt, garlic salt and pepper in bowl until smooth. Add hot potatoes gradually, beating until light and fluffy after each addition. Spoon into 2-quart glass dish. Dot with butter. Microwave on Medium for 5 minutes or until heated through. Sprinkle with paprika.

Peg Hinkle
Monroe, Indiana

POTATO AND CHEESE-STUFFED GREEN PEPPERS

6 green peppers, washed
1 1/2 tsp. salt
3 tbsp. finely chopped onion
1/4 tsp. finely chopped garlic
3 tbsp. bacon drippings
3 c. diced, cooked potatoes
1 c. diced process American cheese
1/2 c. diced celery
4 strips crisp bacon, crumbled
1/4 tsp. pepper
1/2 c. soft bread crumbs

Preheat oven to 350 degrees. Cut thin slice from stem end of each pepper; remove seeds. Place peppers in saucepan with boiling water to cover and 1 teaspoon salt; cover. Bring to a boil; boil for 5 minutes. Remove peppers from water; invert on tray to drain well. Saute onion and garlic in 2 tablespoons bacon drippings for 3 to 4 minutes or until limp. Add next 5 ingredients and remaining salt; mix well. Spoon into peppers. Combine crumbs and remaining bacon drippings. Sprinkle over peppers. Arrange in a close-fitting casserole. Cover. Bake for 30 minutes. Remove cover; bake for 10 minutes longer or until crumbs are brown. Yield: 6 servings.

SUPREME STUFFED POTATOES

4 potatoes
1/2 stick butter

1 sm. onion, grated
1 c. hot evaporated milk
1 tsp. salt
1 tsp. pepper
1/2 c. grated American cheese
Paprika to taste

Bake potatoes at 400 degrees until tender. Cut in halves. Scoop out inside; reserve shells. Mash removed potato; add butter, onion, milk, salt and pepper, beating until fluffy. Fill shells; top with cheese. Sprinkle with paprika. Bake at 400 degrees until lightly browned.

Marie Perdue
Manila, West Virginia

MICROWAVE MEXICAN POTATOES

6 med. potatoes, peeled, sliced
1/2 c. chopped onion
1/2 tsp. garlic salt
1 tsp. instant beef bouillon
1 tsp. salt
2 c. shredded Cheddar cheese
1 4-oz. can chopped green chilies, drained

Combine potatoes, onion, garlic salt, bouillon, salt and 3 tablespoons water in glass dish. Microwave on High for 5 minutes or until potatoes are tender; drain. Layer potatoes, cheese and chilies 1/2 at a time in shallow 2-quart glass dish. Microwave on Medium for 4 to 5 minutes or until heated through. Yield: 6 servings.

Mary Ann Hamm
Castle Rock, Colorado

PARTY SPINACH RING

3 c. cooked spinach
1/2 c. coarse crumbs
1 tsp. onion juice
1 tbsp. chopped celery
1/4 tsp. salt
1/4 tsp. pepper
2 tbsp. margarine, melted
3 eggs, beaten

Combine all ingredients; mix well. Spoon into buttered ring mold; place mold in pan of hot water. Bake at 300 degrees for 30 minutes. Unmold onto large platter; fill ring with creamed cauliflower or mashed potatoes. Surround with garland of buttered sliced carrots. Yield: 6 servings.

Martha June Graber
New Paris, Indiana

MICROWAVING VEGETABLES

Pierce vegetables such as potatoes, squash and tomatoes with thick skins or peels with a fork and cut an X in plastic cooking pouches. This will allow pressure to escape during cooking and improve flavor and texture of vegetables.

Sophia Maneschi
Bridgewater, Virginia

SPINACH TIMBALES

4 slices bacon, diced
1 No. 2 1/2 can spinach, drained
3 eggs, lightly beaten
Salt and pepper to taste
2 tbsp. butter or margarine
2 tbsp. flour
1/2 c. cold milk
1/2 c. hot milk

Fry bacon until crisp; add bacon and bacon grease to spinach, mixing well. Stir in eggs; season with salt and pepper. Fill greased custard cups 2/3 full. Bake at 350 degrees for 40 minutes. Melt butter in top of double boiler; blend in flour. Add cold milk; blend well. Add hot milk. Cook, stirring constantly, until sauce is thickened. Season with salt and pepper. Cover; cook for 5 to 8 minutes. Unmold spinach timbales. Serve with sauce. Yield: 6 servings.

June Houchins
Massillon, Ohio

ECONOMY WITH LEFTOVER VEGETABLES

Keep a large plastic freezer container in freezer. Place leftover vegetables and stock in container as accumulated. Keep frozen. Prepare homemade soup with these vegetables for added flavor and food value.

Mrs. Thelma Kephart
Perry, New York

TEXAS SPINACH-RICE CASSEROLE

2 c. rice, cooked
2 c. chopped frozen spinach, thawed, drained
2 eggs, well beaten
1/2 c. butter, melted
1 c. milk
1 1/2 tsp. salt
1 med. sweet onion, grated
1 c. grated Cheddar cheese

Combine all ingredients in bowl; mix lightly. Pour into buttered casserole. Bake at 300 degrees until set. Yield: 6-8 servings.

Mrs. Marie M. Mingledorff
Douglas, Georgia

SQUASH-CARROT CASSEROLE

2 10-oz. packages frozen squash, cooked, drained
2 med. carrots, grated
1 4-oz. jar pimento, finely chopped
1/2 pt. sour cream
1 can cream of chicken soup
1 pkg. herb stuffing mix
1/4 lb. margarine, melted
Salt and pepper to taste

Mix squash, carrots, pimento, sour cream and soup in saucepan. Mix herb stuffing and margarine in bowl. Line baking dish with half the herb stuffing mixture. Pour in squash mixture; top with remaining herb stuffing mixture. Season with salt and pepper. Bake at 350 degrees for 30 to 40 minutes. Yield: 8 servings.

Mrs. Frank W. Palmer
Gainesville, Florida

GOURMET-BAKED ACORN SQUASH

3 halved acorn squash, seeded
2/3 c. diced celery
1 1/2 c. diced unpeeled apples
1/4 c. butter or margarine
1 1/2 c. soft bread crumbs
1 c. grated American cheese
1/2 tsp. salt
1/8 tsp. pepper

Place squash halves, cut side down, in baking pan in small amount of water. Bake at 400 degrees for 20 to 30 minutes or until almost tender. Saute celery and apples in butter in skillet for 5 minutes; stir in crumbs, cheese, salt and pepper. Turn squash halves; fill with apple mixture. Bake for 10 to 15 minutes longer or until squash halves are tender. Yield: 6 servings.

Mrs. Mary Jo Lyle
Eatonton, Georgia

CHEESE-STUFFED SQUASH

3 yellow crookneck squash
1 1/2 tbsp. butter
2 tbsp. flour
Salt and pepper
1/2 c. milk
1 tbsp. grated onion
4 slices cooked bacon, crumbled
1 c. grated cheese
1/2 c. buttered crumbs

Cook whole squash in boiling water until almost tender; drain. Halve lengthwise; scoop out pulp, reserving pulp and shells. Mash pulp. Melt butter in saucepan over low heat; blend in flour, 1/4 teaspoon salt and dash of pepper. Remove from heat; stir in milk gradually. Return to heat; cook, stirring constantly, until sauce is thickened. Combine sauce, reserved pulp, onion, 3/4 of the bacon and half the cheese; mix well. Season with salt and pepper to taste; spoon into reserved shells. Sprinkle with crumbs, remaining bacon and cheese. Garnish with paprika. Place in shallow baking pan; add small amount of water. Bake at 375 degrees for 25 to 30 minutes or until browned. Yield: 6 servings.

Mrs. Helen Loftin
Denton, North Carolina

ORANGE-CANDIED SWEET POTATOES

6 sweet potatoes, halved
2 tsp. salt
3 tbsp. butter
1 tbsp. orange juice
1/2 tbsp. grated orange rind
3/4 c. corn syrup
1/4 c. (firmly packed) brown sugar

Combine sweet potatoes, salt and 1/2 cup boiling water in saucepan; simmer, covered, for 15 minutes or until sweet potatoes are tender. Pour off all but 1/4 cup stock; dot potatoes with butter. Combine orange juice and rind, corn syrup and brown sugar; blend well. Pour over sweet potatoes. Simmer, basting frequently, for 15 minutes or until glazed, turning once. Yield: 6 servings.

Mrs. Marian G. Craddock
Colorado City, Texas

BANANA-PECAN YAMS

3 c. cooked mashed yams
1 c. pecans, chopped
1/4 c. mashed bananas
1/4 c. butter, softened
1 c. (firmly packed) brown sugar
1/4 tsp. salt
1 tsp. lemon juice
1 tsp. cinnamon

Combine all ingredients; mix until well blended. Pour into 1-quart casserole. Bake at 350 degrees for 30 minutes or until lightly browned. Yield: 6 servings.

Mrs. Catherine Richard
Destrehan, Louisiana

BAKED TOMATO CUPS

3/4 c. bread crumbs
2 tbsp. butter
6 med. tomatoes
1 c. whole kernel corn
3/4 c. mushrooms
1/2 tsp. salt
Pepper to taste

Saute crumbs in butter. Cut thin slice from stem end of each tomato; remove pulp. Reserve 1 cup pulp and shells. Combine reserved tomato pulp, 1/2 cup buttered crumbs, corn, mushrooms, salt and pepper; fill reserved shells. Sprinkle with remaining crumbs; place in baking dish. Bake at 350 degrees for 30 minutes. Yield: 6 servings.

Mrs. Ella Jo Adams
Allen, Texas

FROZEN VEGETABLES FOR ONE OR TWO PERSONS

Buy 10-ounce package frozen peas, lima beans, green beans or corn. Hit side of package on counter sharply enough to separate vegetables. Place amount needed in saucepan; cook according to package directions. Freeze remaining vegetables in package or wrap in plastic wrap, if freezer space is limited.

Mrs. Judith Bibb
Prince Frederick, Maryland

MICROWAVE SUMMER SQUASH SPECIAL

1 lb. yellow squash
1 lb. zucchini
1 2-oz. jar chopped pimento, drained
1/4 tsp. basil
1/4 tsp. garlic powder
1/2 tsp. salt
1/4 tsp. pepper
2 tbsp. butter
2 tbsp. Parmesan cheese

Cut yellow squash and zucchini into 1/2-inch pieces. Combine with pimento, basil, garlic powder, salt, pepper and 2 tablespoons water in 2-quart glass dish. Dot with butter. Microwave, tightly covered with plastic wrap, on High for 9 to 10 minutes or until tender-crisp, stirring twice. Let stand, covered, for 3 minutes. Sprinkle with Parmesan cheese. Yield: 4-6 servings.

Annabel Byers
Salina, Kansas

HOLIDAY VEGETABLE MEDLEY

1 9-oz. package frozen whole green beans
1/2 lb. fresh mushrooms
1 15 1/2-oz. can sm. peeled onions
1/2 c. skim milk
4 tsp. cornstarch
1/4 tsp. ground nutmeg

Cook beans according to package directions. Rinse, pat dry and slice mushrooms; set aside. Drain onions; reserve liquid. Combine skim milk, cornstarch, nutmeg and reserved liquid in saucepan; bring to boiling point, stirring constantly. Reduce heat; add mushrooms and onions. Simmer for 4 to 5 minutes, stirring occasionally. Drain beans. Turn mushroom mixture into serving dish. Surround with hot beans, spooning sauce over beans. One 6 or 8-ounce can sliced mushrooms may be used for fresh mushrooms.

Photograph for this recipe on page 76.

MICROWAVE SPRING VEGETABLE MEDLEY

2 tbsp. butter
8 oz. fresh asparagus, cut into 2-in. pieces
1/2 tsp. basil
1/8 tsp. pepper
8 oz. fresh mushrooms, sliced
1 tomato, cut into wedges
1/2 tsp. salt

Microwave butter in 1 1/2-glass dish on High for 30 seconds or until melted. Add asparagus, basil and pepper; toss lightly. Microwave, tightly covered, for 3 minutes. Add mushrooms; toss lightly. Microwave, covered, for 3 minutes. Stir in tomato. Microwave, covered, for 2 minutes. Stir in salt. Let stand, covered, for 3 minutes.

Florence Morley
Altus, Oklahoma

VEGETABLES IN VINAIGRETTE

1 No. 303 can French-style green beans
1 No. 303 can lge. English peas
1 cucumber, sliced
1 onion, sliced

4 or 5 stalks celery, chopped
1 green pepper, cut into rings
1 red sweet pepper, chopped
2 cans artichoke hearts
1/2 c. corn oil
1 c. vinegar
1/2 to 1 c. sugar
1 tsp. salt

Drain beans and peas. Combine all ingredients in bowl; toss. Refrigerate for 48 hours. Drain; serve. One small jar pimento, drained and chopped, may be substituted for fresh red sweet pepper. Yield: 25 servings.

Mrs. Billie Shreckengaust
Raymondville, Texas

LEFTOVER VEGETABLES A LA CARTE

Fill greased egg-poaching cups with small amounts of different leftover vegetables; heat as for poached eggs. Arrange for serving so diners may select favorite vegetables.

Mrs. Irma Ewing
Mackinaw City, Michigan

MOCK NOODLES ROMANOFF

6 oz. noodles
Salt
1 c. cottage cheese
1 c. sour cream
1 tsp. minced onion
1 sm. clove of garlic, minced
1 tsp. Worcestershire sauce
1/4 c. grated cheese

Cook noodles in boiling salted water until tender; drain. Combine cottage cheese, sour cream and noodles. Add onion, garlic, 1/2 teaspoon salt and Worcestershire sauce. Place in greased 2-quart casserole; sprinkle with cheese. Bake at 350 degrees for 40 minutes. Sour cream may be omitted and cottage cheese increased. Yield: 6 servings.

Myrtle Stevens
Ninnekah, Oklahoma

GREEN AND GOLD RICE

1 pkg. frozen broccoli
1 c. instant rice
2 1/2 c. milk
3/4 tsp. salt
2 c. grated cheese
Dash of pepper
Dash of dry mustard
1/8 tsp. Worcestershire sauce
1/2 c. fine fresh bread crumbs

Cook broccoli according to package directions; drain and set aside. Combine rice, milk and salt in saucepan; mix until rice is softened. Bring quickly to a boil; fluff once or twice with fork. Cover; simmer for 3 minutes. Add cheese, pepper, mustard, Worcestershire sauce and broccoli; blend lightly. Place in greased casserole; sprinkle with bread crumbs. Bake at 350 degrees for 25 minutes. Yield: 6 servings.

Mrs. M. Judelle Jones
Turlock, California

OLD-FASHIONED DUMPLINGS

1 1/2 c. flour
1/2 tsp. salt
3 tbsp. shortening
1 egg, beaten
5 tbsp. water
Broth

Combine flour and salt; cut in shortening. Add egg and water; stir to form soft dough. Turn dough onto floured surface; roll thin. Let dough dry for 20 minutes; cut into thin strips. Drop dough into boiling broth. Cover; cook for about 20 minutes or until dumplings are done. Yield: 6 servings.

Mrs. Vivian Shiver
Magnolia, Arkansas

Breads

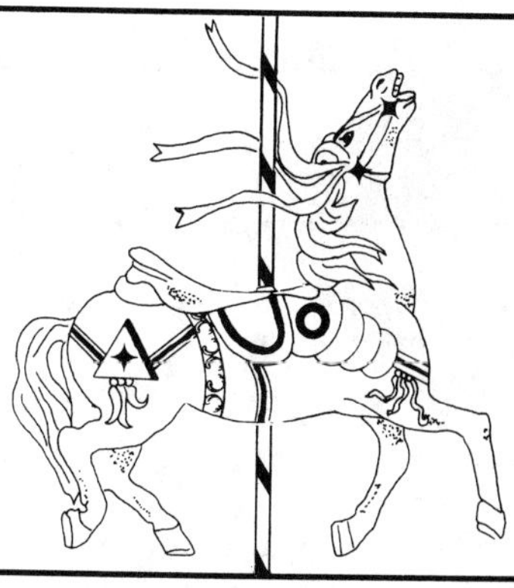

Bread making is a unique joy for every homemaker. No other kitchen activity brings such a sense of accomplishment. Combine this with the money saved by baking your own rye bread, French bread, biscuits, muffins, coffee cakes and sweet rolls, and you will know you have excelled as a thrifty homemaker.

What's more, freshly-baked bread is not only delicious but nutritious as well . . . so important in today's meal planning when we are more conscious than ever before of the need for healthy foods. Because of the variety in this section, you will find yourself turning again and again to these recipes . . . luscious hot biscuits for a family breakfast . . . delicious coffee cake for a brunch . . . and a quick loaf for dinner – certain to please any family.

These recipes have been all-time favorites in homes across the nation for years and will soon become your favorites too. Bread making was never easier on the budget or more fun!

ANGEL BISCUITS

1 pkg. yeast
2 tbsp. lukewarm water
5 to 5 1/2 c. sifted flour
1 tsp. baking soda
3 tsp. baking powder
4 tbsp. sugar
1 tsp. salt
1 c. shortening
2 c. buttermilk

Dissolve yeast in lukewarm water. Sift dry ingredients together. Cut in shortening until crumbly. Add yeast and buttermilk. Knead until dough holds together. Roll 1/2 to 3/4 inch thick on floured surface. Cut with biscuit cutter; fold in half. Place on baking sheet. Bake at 400 degrees for 15 to 20 minutes.

Louise G. Black
Anson, Maryland

MAYONNAISE BISCUITS

2 c. self-rising flour
2 tbsp. mayonnaise
1 c. milk

Combine all ingredients in bowl; mix well. Fill greased and floured muffin cups 2/3 full. Bake at 450 degrees until golden brown.

Mrs. Mary June Sheets
Jefferson, North Carolina

SOUTHERN BISCUITS

2 to 2 1/4 c. flour
1/2 tsp. soda
2 tsp. baking powder
1/2 to 1 tsp. salt
6 tbsp. shortening
2/3 to 1 c. buttermilk

Sift flour, soda, baking powder and salt together in bowl. Cut in shortening until crumbly. Stir in milk to make soft dough. Knead lightly on lightly floured surface. Roll out 1/2 inch thick. Cut with biscuit cutter. Place on lightly greased baking sheet. Bake at 450 degrees for 8 to 10 minutes. Yield: 20.

Helen Barbee
Joliet, Illinois

MICROWAVE BLUEBERRY MUFFINS

2 c. flour
1/2 c. sugar
1 tbsp. baking powder
1/2 tsp. salt
2 eggs, beaten
1/2 c. milk
1/2 c. oil
1/2 c. drained blueberries
Cinnamon-sugar

Sift flour, sugar, baking powder and salt into bowl. Add eggs, milk and oil; mix just until moistened. Stir in blueberries. Fill paper-lined muffin cups 1/2 full. Sprinkle with cinnamon-sugar. Microwave 6 at a time on Medium-High for 2 1/2 to 4 minutes or until muffins test done. Yield: 1 dozen.

Carlene Phillips
Detroit, Michigan

REFRIGERATOR BRAN MUFFINS

5 tsp. soda
2 c. boiling water
1 c. shortening
2 c. sugar
4 eggs
1 qt. buttermilk
4 c. flour
1 tsp. salt
4 c. All-Bran cereal
2 c. 40% bran flakes
2 c. chopped dates

Add soda to boiling water; cool. Cream shortening and sugar. Add eggs and soda mixture. Add remaining ingredients; mix well. Store, covered, in refrigerator for up to six weeks. Do not stir. Spoon into muffin tins. Bake at 375 degrees for 25 minutes.

Winnie Wilson
Blue Point, Maine

RICH MUFFINS

2 c. sifted flour
1/2 c. sugar
1 tbsp. baking powder
1/2 tsp. salt
2 eggs, beaten
1/2 c. cooking oil
1/2 c. milk
1/2 c. chopped nuts or raisins (opt.)

Sift dry ingredients together in bowl; make well in center. Combine next 3 ingredients in bowl; mix well. Add to dry ingredients, stirring until just mixed. Add nuts or raisins. Fill greased muffin cups 2/3 full. Bake at 400 degrees for 15 to 20 minutes or until muffins test done. Yield: 10-12 servings.

Lucille Reid Marker
Robertsdale, Alabama

PANSY'S CORN MUFFINS

1 c. flour, sifted
1/4 c. sugar
3/4 tsp. salt
1 tbsp. baking powder
1 c. cornmeal, sifted
1 egg, well beaten
1 c. milk
5 tbsp. shortening, melted

Sift first 5 ingredients together into bowl. Combine egg, milk and shortening in bowl. Add to dry ingredients, stirring just until mixed. Fill greased muffin cups 2/3 full. Bake at 425 degrees for 20 minutes. Yield: 12.

Pansy Maddox
Vidalia, Georgia

GOLDEN CORN BREAD

1 c. cornmeal
1 c. sifted flour
1/4 c. sugar
1/2 tsp. salt
4 tsp. baking powder
1 egg
1 c. milk
1/4 c. shortening

Sift dry ingredients into bowl; add egg, milk and shortening. Beat with egg beater until smooth; place in greased 8-inch pan. Bake at 425 degrees for 20 to 25 minutes. Yield: 6 servings.

Mrs. William Hamlet
Chattanooga, Tennessee

SPANISH CORN BREAD

1 12-oz. package corn muffin mix
1 12-oz. can whole kernel corn with sweet peppers
1/2 tsp. dry mustard
1 sm. onion, chopped
1 egg, beaten
2/3 c. milk

Combine muffin mix, corn, mustard and onion. Add egg and milk; blend according to package directions. Spread in greased pan. Bake at 400 degrees for 20 minutes or until corn bread tests done. Serve warm.

Mrs. Julia Acker
West Branch, Michigan

JALAPENO CORN BREAD

3 c. corn bread mix
2 1/2 c. milk
1/2 c. salad oil
3 beaten eggs
1 lge. onion, grated
1 c. canned cream-style corn
1 1/2 c. grated yellow cheese
1/2 c. chopped jalapeno peppers

Preheat oven to 400 degrees. Combine all ingredients; mix well. Pour into greased 13 x 9-inch pan. Bake for about 45 minutes.

Edith Donaldson
Anthony, New Mexico

BANANA BREAD

1 c. sugar
1/2 c. shortening
2 eggs
3 bananas, mashed
1 tsp. vanilla extract
2 c. flour
1 tsp. soda
1/2 tsp. salt
1/2 c. chopped pecans

Cream sugar and shortening in bowl; add eggs, bananas and vanilla. Sift flour, soda and salt together. Add to sugar mixture. Fold in nuts. Pour into greased loaf pan. Bake at 350 degrees for 45 minutes to 1 hour.

Mrs. Pansy Gaskill
Fort Worth, Texas

QUICK COFFEE CAKE

2 tsp. baking powder
1 tbsp. butter
1 egg
1 c. sugar
3/4 c. milk
2 c. flour
Brown sugar
Cinnamon

Mix first 6 ingredients in bowl in order given. Place in 9-inch pan. Sprinkle brown sugar and cinnamon to taste over top. Dot with additional butter. Bake in 350-degree oven for about 45 minutes or until golden brown. Yield: 6-8 servings.

Rosalind Smither
Rutland, Vermont

PECAN CRUNCH COFFEE CAKES

1 c. butter
4 3/4 c. sifted flour
1/2 c. (firmly packed) light brown sugar
1 tbsp. cinnamon
1 c. chopped pecans
4 tsp. baking powder
1 tsp. salt
1 3/4 c. sugar
1 tsp. lemon extract
3 eggs
1 c. evaporated milk

Cut 1/4 cup butter into mixture of 3/4 cup flour, brown sugar and cinnamon until crumbly. Stir in pecans; set aside. Sift remaining flour, baking powder and salt together. Cream 3/4 cup butter, sugar and lemon extract in large bowl. Add eggs 1 at a time, beating well after each addition. Add dry ingredients alternately with evaporated milk, mixing well after each addition. Divide batter evenly between three greased 9-inch round cake pans. Sprinkle topping over batter. Bake at 350 degrees for 20 to 35 minutes. Yield: 3 coffee cakes.

ORANGE-HONEY BUNS

1 recipe biscuit dough
3 tbsp. sugar
1 tsp. cinnamon
5 tbsp. margarine, melted
2 tbsp. orange juice
1 tsp. orange rind
1/2 c. honey
1/2 c. chopped nuts

Roll biscuit dough into 1/4-inch thick rectangle on floured surface. Combine sugar and cinnamon. Brush 1 tablespoon melted margarine over biscuit dough. Sprinkle with mixture of sugar and cinnamon. Roll tightly as for jelly roll; set aside. Mix orange juice, orange rind, honey and 1/4 cup margarine in bowl. Pour into 8-inch square cake pan. Sprinkle chopped nuts over top. Cut dough into 16 slices. Place, cut-side down, on orange and honey mixture. Bake at 375 degrees for 25 minutes or until brown. Invert onto serving plate immediately after removing from oven. Serve hot. Yield: 8 servings.

Mrs. Jean Fancher
Bronte, Texas

VARIED USES FOR REFRIGERATOR BISCUITS

Canned refrigerator biscuits, which are very economical, may be used in a variety of ways, such as cutting in shapes or rolling thin for pizza crust.

Mrs. Edna Schieber
Barnard, Missouri

POPOVERS

2 eggs, beaten
1 c. milk
1 tbsp. melted shortening
1 c. sifted all-purpose flour
1/2 tsp. salt

Combine eggs, milk and shortening. Add flour and salt; beat with hand beater until mixture is smooth and free of lumps. Pour into hot, oiled custard cups or iron muffin pans, filling half full. Bake for 40 minutes at 425 degrees. One-fourth cup grated sharp Cheddar cheese may be added, if desired. Yield: 8-12 servings.

Mrs. Marjorie West
Lauderdale, Mississippi

PREPARING HERB-SEASONED BREAD CRUMBS

Dry leftover bread slices in 250-degree oven until crisp but not brown. Break up dried bread; place in blender container. Blend at medium speed until fine crumbs are formed. Bread may be placed in a bag and rolled with rolling pin. Stir 1 cup crumbs with 1 tablespoon oregano, 1/2 teaspoon thyme, 1/2 teaspoon onion salt and 1/8 teaspoon pepper to make seasoned crumbs. Homemade mixture is much less expensive than packaged mix. Store, covered, in dry place or freeze.

Evelyn B. Willey
Gatesville, North Carolina

GARLIC BREAD STICKS

Bread slices
1/4 c. butter, melted
Garlic powder to taste
3/4 to 1 c. cereal, crushed

Cut bread slices into 1-inch strips. Mix butter and garlic powder in bowl. Dip bread sticks into butter mixture; roll in crushed cereal. Place on baking sheet. Bake at 350 degrees for 5 minutes. Turn to brown both sides.

Ione Kjos
Wyndmere, North Dakota

ONION BREAD

1 loaf French-style bread
5 to 7 scallions, chopped
1/4 lb. butter, softened

Cut loaf lengthwise. Mix scallions and butter; spread on loaf. Wrap in foil. Bake at 400 degrees for 20 minutes. Yield: 4-6 servings.

LaVonne Geisler
Carlisle, Iowa

FOR BETTER-TASTING DOUGHNUTS

A small amount of vinegar added to deep fat while heating to fry doughnuts will eliminate any greasy taste in doughnuts.

Anne Michaud
Edmundston, New Brunswick, Canada

LIGHT DOUGHNUTS

4 tsp. baking powder
1/2 tsp. nutmeg
1 tsp. salt
3 1/2 c. flour
1 egg
2 egg yolks
1 c. milk
1 c. sugar
3 tbsp. melted butter, cooled
Oil for deep frying
Cinnamon-sugar

Sift baking powder, nutmeg, salt and flour together. Beat egg and egg yolks in bowl. Add milk, sugar and butter; mix well. Add sifted ingredients; stir until combined. Knead lightly on floured surface; roll out 1/4 inch thick. Cut with doughnut cutter. Fry in deep hot oil at 370 degrees until brown, turning once. Roll in cinnamon-sugar while warm.

Mary K. Rattan
Odessa, Texas

YEAST DOUGHNUTS

2 c. lukewarm milk
Sugar
1 1/2 tsp. salt
2 pkg. yeast
1/2 c. lukewarm water
1/2 c. shortening, melted
2 eggs
Flour
1/2 tsp. cinnamon
1/4 tsp. nutmeg
Oil for deep frying
1 box powdered sugar
1/2 tsp. vanilla extract

Combine milk, 2/3 cup sugar and 1 teaspoon salt in bowl. Dissolve yeast in water and 1/2 teaspoon sugar. Combine milk and yeast mixtures with shortening and eggs. Add enough flour, sifted with cinnamon and nutmeg, to make soft dough. Place in large bowl; cover with damp cloth. Let rise until doubled in size. Punch down; let rise again. Roll out dough 1/3 inch thick on floured surface. Cut doughnuts; place on floured board to rise. Let rise, uncovered, for 45 minutes. Fry in deep hot oil until golden brown. Drain on paper towels. Combine remaining ingredients and 1/2 teaspoon salt with enough water to make glaze in bowl; mix well. Drizzle over doughnuts.

Mrs. William Cooke
Bainbridge, Georgia

NEVER-FAIL DUMPLINGS

2 c. sifted flour
3 tsp. baking powder
1/2 tsp. salt
1 tbsp. shortening
3/4 c. milk
Chicken broth

Sift flour with baking powder and salt into bowl. Cut in shortening until crumbly. Add enough milk to make drop batter. Drop by spoonfuls into boiling stock in saucepan. Cover tightly. Cook for 10 minutes. Yield: 6 servings.

Mable Wilson
Krafton, Wyoming

FREEZING APPLES FOR FUTURE USE

Peel, quarter and slice apples a few at a time; drop immediately into cold lightly salted water. Dip apples from water; place in freezer container. Freeze quickly. Salt water prevents apples from darkening.

Mrs. Lila Akes
Leon, Iowa

APPLE PANCAKES

1 c. sifted flour
1/2 tsp. baking powder
Pinch of salt
1 c. milk
5 eggs
5 tbsp. melted butter
Powdered sugar
3 apples, sliced

Sift dry ingredients together in bowl. Stir in milk. Add eggs, 1 at a time, beating well after each addition. Add 2 tablespoons butter; pour batter into hot greased skillet. Cook over medium heat for 1 minute. Bake at 425 degrees for 20 to 25 minutes or until browned, puffed and curled up at edges. Sprinkle with powdered sugar. Saute apples in remaining butter; serve with pancakes.

Mrs. Marinda Craiger
Ironton, Ohio

RICE DOLLAR PANCAKES

1 c. sifted flour
1 tsp. baking powder
1/2 tsp. soda
1/4 tsp. salt
1 tsp. sugar
1 c. buttermilk
3 tbsp. melted butter
2 eggs, separated
1/2 c. cooked rice

Sift together dry ingredients. Add milk and butter to beaten egg yolks; mix well. Stir in dry ingredients; beat just until smooth. Add rice. Fold in stiffly beaten egg whites. Drop by tablespoonfuls onto hot griddle. Bake until browned on both sides. Yield: 3 dozen.

Photograph for this recipe on page 92.

PUFF PANCAKES WITH STRAWBERRIES AND SOUR CREAM

2 eggs
1 c. milk
2 1/3 c. biscuit mix
2 tbsp. sugar
1/4 c. cooking oil
1/2 pt. sour cream
1 10-oz. package frozen strawberries, thawed

Beat eggs in bowl until soft peaks form; blend in milk. Add biscuit mix and sugar; stir just until thoroughly dampened. Fold in oil. Drop by spoonfuls onto medium-hot griddle. Cook until puffed and bubbles begin to break; turn. Cook on other side. Arrange on large platter; spoon sour cream and strawberries over pancakes. Yield: 18 servings.

Lucille Patton
Butte, Montana

RESTORE BROWN SUGAR

Replace the moisture in brown sugar by placing sugar in an airtight container with a piece of apple, slice of bread or small piece of lettuce.

Norine Brewster
Pottsboro, New Hampshire

MICROWAVE BOSTON BROWN BREAD

1 c. buttermilk
1/2 c. molasses
1/2 c. raisins
1/2 tsp. baking powder
1/2 tsp. soda
1/2 tsp. salt
1/2 c. whole wheat flour
1/4 c. flour
1/2 c. yellow cornmeal

Combine buttermilk and molasses in bowl; mix well. Add raisins, baking powder, soda and salt; mix well. Add whole wheat flour, flour and cornmeal; mix just until moistened. Pour into greased 4-cup glass measure. Cover loosely with plastic wrap; secure with rubber band. Microwave on Medium for 8 1/2 to 9 1/2 minutes or just until set. Let stand, uncovered, for 10 minutes. Remove from measure. Let stand for 5 minutes longer before slicing. Yield: 8 servings.

Jane E. Cooley
Lynnwood, Washington

IRISH FRECKLE BREAD

2 pkg. yeast
1 c. warm potato water
1/4 c. mashed potatoes
8 tbsp. sugar
2 to 3 c. sifted flour
1 tbsp. salt
2 eggs, beaten
1/2 c. shortening, melted
1 c. raisins

Dissolve yeast in potato water in bowl. Add mashed potatoes, 2 tablespoons sugar and 1 cup flour to make a sponge. Let rise, covered, for 30 minutes. Beat until smooth. Add salt, eggs, shortening,raisins and enough flour to make soft dough. Knead on lightly floured board until smooth and elastic. Place in greased bowl, turning to grease surface. Let rise, covered, for about 1 hour. Punch down; divide into 4 equal parts. Let rest, covered, for 5 minutes. Shape each section into roll 1 1/2 inches in diameter. Place in pairs with sides touching in greased loaf pans. Let rise for 1 hour. Bake at 350 degrees for 1 hour. Yield: 2 loaves.

Sandra Jane Edwards
Irving, Texas

MICROWAVE ENGLISH MUFFIN BREAD

4 1/4 c. flour
1 c. wheat bran cereal
2 pkg. dry yeast
1 tbsp. sugar
2 tsp. salt
1/4 tsp. soda
2 c. milk
Cornmeal

Combine 2 1/2 cups flour, bran cereal, yeast, sugar, salt and soda in large bowl. Heat milk and 1/2 cup water to 130 degrees in saucepan. Add to dry ingredients; mix well. Stir in enough remaining flour to make a stiff batter. Sprinkle cornmeal into 2 greased 4 x 8-inch microwave loaf pans. Spoon batter into pans; sprinkle with additional cornmeal. Let rise, covered, in warm place for 45 minutes. Microwave 1 loaf at a time on High for 6 1/2 minutes. Let stand for 5 minutes. Slice and toast to serve. Yield: 16 servings.

Susan O'Connor
Aniston, Georgia

SOUR CREAM COFFEE CAKE

1 pkg. dry yeast
1/4 c. warm water
3/4 c. sour cream
2 tbsp. shortening
1 egg
3 c. flour
1/8 tsp. soda
3 tbsp. sugar
1/8 tsp. salt
2 tbsp. butter, softened
1 c. (firmly packed) brown sugar
1 tsp. cinnamon
Confectioners' sugar

Dissolve yeast in 1/4 cup warm water in bowl. Add sour cream, shortening and egg. Sift next 4 dry ingredients together. Combine with sour cream mixture. Place in greased bowl. Let rise until doubled in bulk. Roll out on floured surface into 1/2-inch thick rectangle. Combine next 3 ingredients in bowl. Spread over half the dough. Fold remaining half over to enclose filling. Cut into 1-inch strips; twist. Place on baking sheet. Let rise until doubled in bulk. Bake at 375 degrees for 12 to 15 minutes. Mix confectioners' sugar with enough water in bowl to make glaze. Spread over cake. Yield: 12 servings.

Mrs. Merle G. Hail
Eunice, Louisiana

YEAST ROLLS

1 c. milk, scalded
1/4 c. sugar
1 tsp. salt
Margarine
1/2 c. warm water
2 pkg. active dry yeast
2 eggs, beaten
5 1/4 c. flour

Combine milk, sugar, salt and 1/4 cup margarine. Cool to lukewarm. Measure warm water into large warm bowl. Add yeast; stir until dissolved. Add lukewarm milk mixture, eggs and 2 cups flour; beat until smooth. Stir in enough additional flour to make soft dough. Turn out onto lightly floured board; knead until smooth and elastic. Place in greased bowl, turning to grease top. Cover; let rise in warm place until doubled in bulk, about 30 minutes. Punch down. Turn out on lightly floured board. Shape as desired. Place on baking sheet. Let rise until doubled in bulk. Brush with melted margarine. Bake at 400 degrees for 12 to 15 minutes or until brown. Yield: 24-36 rolls.

BATTER ROLLS

1 pkg. yeast
2 c. warm water
1/2 c. shortening, melted
1/3 c. sugar
1 1/2 tsp. salt
1 tsp. baking powder
1/4 tsp. soda
5 c. sifted flour

Dissolve yeast in warm water in large bowl. Add lukewarm shortening and sugar; mix well. Add salt, baking powder, soda and flour. Stir until well mixed. Let rise in warm place until doubled in bulk; stir. Refrigerate for several hours or longer. Shape into rolls. Place on greased pan. Let rise for about 1 hour. Bake at 350 degrees until lightly browned. Yield: 24 rolls.

Mrs. Leon Potts
Kossuth, Mississippi

CITRUS PEEL STORAGE

Grate rinds of lemons, oranges or other citrus fruits; place in jar. Cover tightly; store in refrigerator. Use for adding dash of flavor to appropriate dishes.

Mrs. Lewis Vance
Jefferson, Pennsylvania

QUICK BUTTER FLUFF ROLLS

1 pkg. dry yeast
1/4 c. warm water
1 c. lukewarm buttermilk
1/4 c. sugar
1 tsp. salt
1/2 tsp. soda
1/4 c. butter, softened
2 eggs
4 to 4 1/2 c. sifted flour
Butter, melted

Soak yeast in warm water in bowl for 5 minutes. Combine buttermilk, sugar, salt, soda, butter, eggs, yeast mixture and half the flour in mixing bowl. Beat with electric mixer for 2 minutes. Stir in remaining flour to make soft dough. Turn onto lightly floured board. Knead until smooth and elastic. Roll dough into 10 x 6-inch oblong. Cut into 6 long strips. Spread with softened butter. Stack 3 strips of dough. Cut into twelve 1 1/2-inch cubes. Repeat with remaining dough. Place in greased muffin cups. Brush with melted butter. Let rise, covered, for 45 to 60 minutes. Bake at 425 degrees until golden brown. Yield: 2 dozen.

Linda Chaviers
New Caney, Texas

ICEBOX ROLLS

1 qt. milk
1 c. sugar
1 c. mashed potatoes
1 c. melted shortening
2 pkg. yeast
12 c. flour
1 tsp. salt
2 tsp. baking powder
1 tsp. soda

Scald milk; cool to lukewarm. Combine sugar and potatoes in large mixing bowl; mix well. Add milk and shortening; stir in yeast. Sift 6 cups flour, salt, baking powder and soda together; stir into yeast mixture. Cover dough; let rise for 2 hours. Punch dough down; work in remaining flour. Cover; refrigerate overnight. Shape dough into rolls; place in greased baking pans. Let rise until almost doubled in bulk. Bake at 400 degrees for about 15 minutes or until browned.

Mrs. Betty Peters
Inkster, Michigan

BUTTERHORN ROLLS

1 pkg. yeast
1/2 c. sugar

1/2 c. shortening
1 tsp. salt
2 eggs
4 c. sifted flour
Melted butter

Soften yeast in 3 tablespoons warm water. Combine sugar, shortening, 1 cup warm water, salt and eggs in large bowl; mix well. Add yeast and flour; beat until smooth. Cover; refrigerate overnight. Roll dough into circle; spread with butter. Cut into 16 triangles. Roll triangles up, beginning with wide end; place on greased baking sheet, point side down. Let rise until doubled in bulk. Bake at 350 degrees until brown.

Mrs. Jeannette Crouse
O'Fallon, Utah

FRESH BREAD EVERY DAY FOR SMALL FAMILIES

Frozen unbaked small bread loaves are available in store freezers. Purchase these loaves and bake, one at a time, for 2 to 3-member families instead of buying the usual loaf which, because of the quantity of bread, frequently becomes quite stale before being completely used.

Mrs. Eloise Thorson
Hicks, Louisiana

ONION ROLLS

1 pkg. yeast
1 c. milk
2 tbsp. sugar
1 1/2 tsp. salt
1/2 c. margarine
3 1/2 c. sifted flour
4 med. onions, sliced
1 egg, beaten
1/4 c. sour cream
1 tbsp. poppy seed

Soften yeast in 1/4 cup warm water. Scald milk; pour into large bowl. Add sugar, 1 teaspoon salt and 1/4 cup margarine. Stir to melt margarine; cool to lukewarm. Add yeast and 2 1/2 cups flour; beat until smooth. Work in remaining flour. Cover; let rise for 1 hour or until doubled in bulk. Saute onions in remaining margarine until tender. Cool. Combine egg, sour cream and remaining salt; mix well. Turn dough onto floured surface; knead lightly. Shape into 12-inch long roll; cut into 12 parts. Shape each part to a ball; flatten balls on greased baking sheet. Press onions into tops of rolls; spread with sour cream mixture. Sprinkle with poppy seed. Let rise for about 45 minutes. Bake at 375 degrees for 25 minutes.

Ellen F. Dow
Windsor, Vermont

ICEBOX BUNS

1 pkg. yeast
1 tsp. salt
5 c. (about) flour
1 c. lard
1 c. sugar
2 eggs, beaten

Dissolve yeast in 2 cups warm water; add salt and enough flour to make thin batter. Beat until smooth. Let rise for about 2 hours. Cream lard and sugar together; beat in eggs. Add sponge and 1 cup cold water. Add enough remaining flour to make soft dough; chill. Form into buns; place in greased baking pans. Let rise for 30 minutes. Bake at 375 degrees until lightly browned.

Peggy Frost
Esbon, Kansas

CRUSTY MICROWAVE BREADS

To form a "crust" on microwaved yeast breads, brush with milk or melted butter, then sprinkle generously with one of the following before rising: wheat germ; fine bread or cracker crumbs; crumbs mixed with Parmesan cheese; crumbs mixed with herbs; or crumbs mixed with sesame, caraway seed or poppy seed.

Ruth Voegli
Charleston, South Carolina

Desserts

Thrifty homemakers know that desserts derive their excitement not from expensive ingredients but from the imagination that goes into their making. Cakes with surprise fillings and melt-in-the-mouth frostings . . . creamy smooth puddings . . . richly flavorful pies . . . an endless variety of wonderful ways to end every meal with a flourish.

The creative world of desserts is captured for you in the section that follows. From the recipe files of America's thriftiest homemakers come tried-and-proven favorites – and each one has been chosen not just for its delicious flavor but for its low cost as well. Now, for just pennies a serving, you can end every meal with an extra-special treat.

To stretch your food dollar even further, we've included household hints from these same thrifty women. Learn their secrets for substitutions and shortcuts that save dollars every month. You'll find many fascinating ways to trim your food budget – without sacrificing flavor excitement!

As you read through the pages that follow, you'll find yourself imagining your family's pleasure in a delicious dessert – at just pennies a serving!

Desserts

GETTING MORE FOR YOUR MONEY

A dessert is the just-right ending to every meal. It may be fruit . . . cake . . . pie . . . a tart . . . but whatever it is, it is a match for what has gone before. Knowing what to look for in the dessert you serve is a smart way to save on food dollars.

FRUIT

Fresh fruit, in season, is one of the most economical and most delicious desserts you can find. Be sure to store your ripe fruit in the refrigerator – ripe fruit stored at room temperature quickly loses its vitamins A, B, and C. Similarly, there is more vitamin loss in bruised or soft fruit than in just-ripe, carefully handled pieces.

Apples, if locally grown, are usually an excellent buy. Local fruit is generally tree-ripened and has better flavor and more vitamins. Fruit trucked in from a distance may have been forced to ripen and will have lost flavor and nutrients during its travels.

Oranges, grapefruit, and other *citrus fruit* should be just barely firm and have a thin skin. Avoid rough, thick-skinned fruit. Color is not a guide to quality – almost all fruit is artificially colored by the growers.

Peaches should be slightly soft when you buy them. Here, too, color is not a guide to quality. The peach with the pinkest blush may also be the hardest inside. When peeling peaches for desserts, don't soak them in water. Water destroys vitamins B and C. Instead, hold them over steam and then peel quickly.

Pears are an almost classic dessert fruit. Served with cheese, they are a perfect finish to a heavy and filling meal. The best pears yield to pressure at the base of their stem.

Strawberries should be bright red and have their caps. During the height of the season, strawberries will come into your store daily. Don't depend on the store's produce department to put the fresh berries on top – many times they will try to move the older stock first by putting boxes of fresh berries on the bottom of the stack.

Bananas are a year-round good buy. When they are black or have brown spots, many grocery stores will give them away. The color of the skin does not affect the quality of the actual banana – those with discolored skins are wonderful to use in cooking.

Don't overlook *canned fruit.* When your supermarket has a special on canned fruit in several flavors, buy one of each and mix them into an elegant fruit compote. Nutrition and flavor, for just pennies a serving.

When buying canned fruit, calculate cost per serving to determine which can is the best buy. An eight-ounce can serves two, a sixteen-ounce can serves three or four. A number 303 can also serves three to four; number two can, four to five; number two and a half can, six to seven; and number three can, eight to twelve. Dented cans are frequently marked down at your grocery store – and there is seldom anything wrong with them. However, a can which is swollen at either end or is leaking is no bargain – the food in it is usually spoiled.

OTHER DESSERTS

Of all the desserts you can prepare, none is so elegant – or economical – as *crepes.* They save you time, too. The crepe itself, a pancake, can be prepared ahead of time and wrapped tightly in foil. These packages can be kept in the refrigerator for days or in the freezer for months. When you're ready to serve them, heat gently in butter until warm.

Crepes are wrapped around any one of many fillings. Some of the fillings you can prepare easily – and inexpensively – are bananas . . . jam . . . strawberries . . . pineapple . . . apple . . . peach . . . chocolate. It takes less than a tablespoon of filling per crepe – a delicious bargain to end your meals with an extra-special touch.

Tarts and pies are always welcome desserts. Many times, you can save time and money by purchasing frozen pies. Grocery stores frequently feature frozen pies at two, three, or four for $2.00. Depending on the size and the type of filling, you'll save lots by purchasing these. Cream pies and out-of-season fruit pies are great buys.

Another boon is the surplus store – the outlet store operated by commercial bakeries in your area. They sell bakery-prepared pies that are a day old for half price or less. Pop one of these fruit pies in the oven and serve it to your family – they'll have trouble telling it from your home-baked pies!

Tarts are something you can prepare yourself for just pennies a serving. You may want to fix your own tart crust. Or, to save time, try the pre-packaged mixes. Tart dough should be richer than the usual pie crust, so add 2 tablespoons of butter and one egg yolk to a package of mix. The result will be crumbly-rich and delicious tart shells ready to be filled with your favorite creamy or fruit filling.

Another quick and easy dessert that's a family favorite is *ice cream sundaes.* Leftover ice cream, sauces, syrups, nuts, and whipped toppings can be combined into favorite desserts everyone will enjoy.

STORED CAKES WITH JUST-BAKED TEXTURE

One half cup mayonnaise or salad dressing beaten into cake batter will insure cake remaining moist and tender throughout storage. This is unusually successful with cakes prepared from mixes. Flavor of cakes is not altered by addition of mayonnaise or salad dressing.

Marilyn Mancewicz
Grand Rapids, Michigan

BANANA LAYER CAKE

6 ripe bananas, mashed
Sugar
1 1/2 tsp. vanilla
2/3 c. shortening
2 1/4 c. sifted cake flour
3 1/4 tsp. baking powder
1 tsp. salt
Milk
2 eggs

Combine bananas, 1/2 cup sugar and 1/2 teaspoon vanilla; mix well. Soften shortening in large electric mixer bowl. Combine flour, baking powder, salt and 1 2/3 cups sugar in sifter; sift over shortening. Add 3/4 cup milk and remaining vanilla. Blend at low speed of mixer; beat for 2 minutes. Add eggs and 6 tablespoons milk; beat for 1 minute longer. Spread 3 tablespoons batter into each of several greased and floured layer pans. Bake at 350 degrees for 10 minutes or until layers test done. Remove layers from pans immediately. Spread with banana mixture and stack onto plate. Repeat until all batter is baked. Serve warm. Yield: 12 servings.

Mrs. Lloyd Smittle
Laneburg, Arkansas

BLUEBERRY CAKE

1/2 c. butter
1 c. flour
1 c. sugar
1/4 tsp. salt
1 tbsp. baking powder
2/3 c. milk
1 can blueberry pie filling

Melt butter in baking dish. Mix remaining ingredients except pie filling. Pour into baking dish; mix. Pour pie filling into center of batter. Do not stir. Bake at 350 degrees for 45 minutes or until brown.

Mary R. Abney
Bay Springs, Mississippi

QUICK CAKE DECORATING HINT

Place a paper doily on top of slightly cooled cake. Sprinkle confectioners' sugar over cake. Remove the doily, revealing an attractive, lacy design.

Mrs. Edith Blasi
Odessa, Texas

CARROT-PECAN CAKE

2 c. sifted flour
2 tsp. baking powder
1 tsp. soda
1 1/2 tsp. salt
1 1/4 c. salad oil
3 c. sugar
4 eggs
3 c. grated carrots
1 c. finely chopped pecans
1/4 c. cornstarch
1 tsp. lemon juice
1 c. orange juice
2 tbsp. grated orange peel
2 tbsp. butter

Sift flour, baking powder, soda and 1 teaspoon salt together. Combine oil and 2 cups sugar in mixing bowl; beat until blended. Beat in half the flour mixture and eggs. Add remaining flour mixture; mix until smooth. Stir in carrots and pecans. Turn batter into greased 10-inch tube pan. Bake at 325 degrees for 1 hour and 10 minutes or until cake tests done. Cool cake in pan. Remove from pan and split into 3 layers. Combine cornstarch, remaining sugar and remaining salt in saucepan; stir in remaining ingredients. Cook over low heat until thickened, stirring constantly. Cool glaze slightly; spread between layers and on top and side of cake.

Mrs. Thelma Randall
Burkeville, Texas

MICROWAVE CHOCOLATE CAKE

1/4 c. baking cocoa
1 c. cake flour
1 c. sugar
1/2 tsp. soda
1/4 tsp. baking powder
1/4 tsp. salt
6 tbsp. oil
1 egg
2 tsp. vanilla

Grease 8-inch round glass cake pan; line bottom with waxed paper. Combine cocoa and 1/3 cup hot water in glass dish. Microwave on High for 30 to 40 seconds or until very hot and slightly thickened. Combine flour, sugar, soda, baking powder and salt. Add oil, egg, vanilla, 1/3 cup hot water and chocolate mixture; beat with spoon for 40 to 50 strokes or until smooth. Spoon into prepared pan. Microwave on High for 5 to 6 minutes or until cake begins to pull away from side of pan; moist spots will cook during standing time. Let stand for 5 minutes. Invert onto serving plate. Peel off paper. Cool completely. Frost as desired.

Janet Montgomery
Boston, Massachusetts

CHOCOLATE-MAYONNAISE CAKE

2 c. flour
1 c. sugar
1/2 c. cocoa
2 tsp. soda
1 c. mayonnaise or salad dressing
1 c. boiling water
1 tsp. vanilla

Sift flour, sugar, cocoa and soda together 3 times. Combine remaining ingredients in mixing bowl; beat for 2 minutes. Add flour mixture; beat until smooth. Turn batter into 2 greased 8-inch layer pans. Bake at 350 degrees for 45 minutes.

Clariece Seachord
Chester, Nebraska

MICROWAVE ORANGE BLOSSOM CAKE

1/3 c. melted butter
3/4 c. orange marmalade
1/2 c. coconut
1 2-layer package yellow cake mix
3 eggs

Grease glass bundt pan; sprinkle with sugar. Combine butter, marmalade and coconut in glass measure. Microwave on High until butter is melted; mix well. Spread evenly in pan. Combine cake mix, eggs and 1 cup water in mixer bowl. Beat at high speed for 2 minutes. Pour into prepared pan. Microwave on Medium for 13 to 16 minutes, turning pan after 9 minutes. Let stand for 10 minutes. Remove to wire rack to cool.

Pat Koziar
Dayton, Ohio

MICROWAVE CAKE MAGIC

Chill cake mix batter in the refrigerator for one day before cooking it in the microwave. The primary action of the baking powder is diffused and the secondary action, activated by the heat, causes the cake to rise more evenly in the microwave. Cakes will also bake more evenly in a tube pan in the microwave. You can make your own microwave tube pan by inverting a glass or custard cup in a glass casserole.

Hannah James
Tulsa, Oklahoma

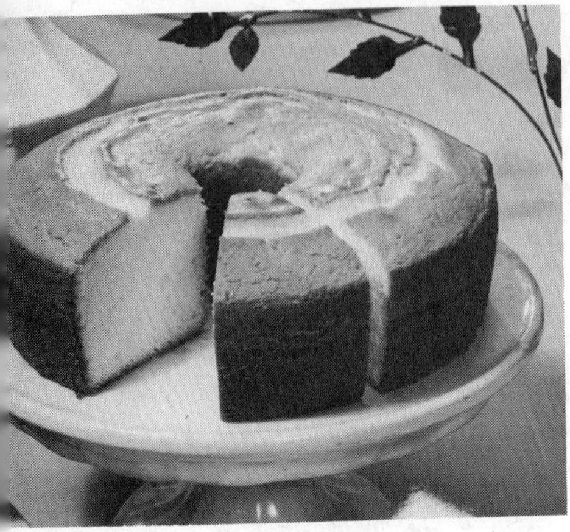

MOCK POUND CAKE

1/2 c. margarine
1 8-oz. package cream cheese
1 1/2 c. sugar
3 eggs, beaten
1 tsp. vanilla
3 c. sifted self-rising cake flour
1/3 c. milk

Blend margarine and cream cheese together in mixing bowl. Add sugar gradually; beat until well mixed. Add eggs, one at a time, blending until smooth; add vanilla. Stir in flour alternately with milk, beginning and ending with flour. Mix until smooth after each addition. Pour into greased and floured 10 x 4-inch tube pan. Bake at 350 degrees for about 1 hour and 10 minutes or until cake tests done.

FREEZING BAKED PRODUCTS IN SMALL PACKAGES

Divide tea rings, cookies and cakes into packages of only a few servings for small families; freeze. A variety of desserts is possible with this method.

Louise Paxton
Blair, Oklahoma

MICROWAVE SPICED CARROT CAKE

1 3/4 c. sifted flour
1 tsp. each baking powder and soda
1/2 tsp. each cinnamon, nutmeg and salt
1 c. oil
1 c. sliced carrots
1 c. sugar
2 eggs
1/2 c. orange juice
1 tsp. vanilla
1/2 c. raisins

Sift flour, baking powder, soda, spices and salt into large bowl. Combine oil and carrots in blender container; process for 30 seconds. Add sugar, eggs, orange juice and vanilla; process for 10 seconds. Add to dry ingredients; mix well. Stir in raisins. Pour into ungreased glass tube pan. Microwave on Medium for 10 minutes, turning pan 1/4 turn every 3 minutes. Microwave on High for 3 minutes or until cake tests done. Let stand for 5 minutes. Remove to wire rack to cool. Frost with cream cheese frosting.

Ruth L. Metcalf
Oviedo, Florida

THRIFTY CAKE

2 c. sugar
1 c. lard
2 c. raisins
1 tsp. cinnamon
2 c. hot water
1/4 tsp. salt
4 c. sifted flour
1 tbsp. soda

Combine sugar, lard, raisins, cinnamon, hot water and salt in saucepan; bring to a boil. Reduce heat; simmer for 3 minutes. Sift flour and soda together; add to hot mixture. Beat until smooth. Turn batter into greased and floured 13 x 9 x 2-inch pan. Bake at 350 degrees for 50 minutes.

Mrs. Kylie Dunkin
Wood River, Nebraska

CREAMY CARROT FUDGE

1 1/2 c. grated carrots
3 1/2 c. sugar
1/2 c. sweetened condensed milk
1/2 c. water
1/2 tsp. lemon flavoring

Mix carrots, sugar, milk and water in saucepan; cook to soft-ball stage. Remove from heat. Add lemon flavoring; mix well. Cool. Beat until creamy; pour into buttered pan. Cool; cut into squares.

Esther Engelhardt
Mt. Pleasant, Iowa

CREAMY MARSHMALLOW FUDGE

1 lge. jar marshmallow creme
1 8-oz. Hershey bar, crushed
1 12-oz. package chocolate chips
1 lge. can evaporated milk
1 c. butter
4 1/2 c. sugar
Chopped pecans to taste (opt.)

Mix marshmallow creme, Hershey bar and chocolate chips in large bowl; set aside. Mix milk, butter and sugar in saucepan; bring to a boil. Boil for 5 minutes, stirring constantly. Pour over ingredients in bowl; beat until chocolate is melted. Add pecans; mix well. Pour into well-greased 9 x 12-inch pan. Chill overnight. Cut into squares.

Ardith Wakefield
Darien, Illinois

MICROWAVE SUPER EASY FUDGE

1 lb. confectioners' sugar
1/4 tsp. salt
1/2 c. baking cocoa
1/4 c. evaporated milk
1 stick margarine, sliced
1 tbsp. vanilla
1/2 c. chopped pecans

Sift confectioners' sugar, salt and cocoa into 3-quart glass dish. Add milk; mix just until moistened. Top with margarine; do not stir. Microwave on High for 2 minutes. Add vanilla. Beat until smooth. Stir in pecans. Pour into buttered 8 x 8-inch dish. Chill for 1 hour or longer. Cut into squares. Yield: 36 servings.

Lucinda Whitley
Lamar, Arkansas

QUICK PEANUT FUDGE

2 c. sugar
3 tbsp. butter
1 c. evaporated milk
1 c. miniature marshmallows
1 12-oz. jar chunk-style peanut butter
1 tsp. vanilla

Combine sugar, butter and milk in electric skillet. Set thermostat at 280 degrees. Bring mixture to a boil; boil for 5 minutes, stirring constantly. Turn off skillet. Add marshmallows, peanut butter and vanilla. Stir until marshmallows and peanut butter are melted and blended. Pour into buttered 8-inch square pan. Cool. Cut into squares. Yield: About 2 pounds candy.

WHIPPED CREAM SWIRLS

Make whipped cream swirls on cookie sheet using leftover whipping cream. Place cookie sheet in freezer until swirls are firm. Remove from cookie sheet; wrap in plastic wrap. Store in freezer until needed.

Mrs. Betty Ambrose
Midland, Texas

MICROWAVE ROCKY ROAD FUDGE

12 oz. chocolate chips
1 c. peanut butter
1/2 c. butter
3 c. miniature marshmallows

Combine chocolate chips, peanut butter and butter in 9 x 9-inch glass dish. Microwave on High for 1 to 2 minutes or until melted; mix well. Stir in marshmallows. Chill in refrigerator. Cut into squares. Yield: 36 servings.

Jeanne Flude
Saskatchewan, Canada

MICROWAVE PECAN BRITTLE

1 c. sugar
1/2 c. light corn syrup
1 c. pecans
1 tsp. vanilla
1 tbsp. butter
1 tsp. soda

Mix sugar and corn syrup in glass dish. Microwave on High for 4 minutes. Stir in pecans. Microwave for 3 minutes. Stir in vanilla and butter. Microwave for 2 minutes. Stir in soda. Pour into buttered dish. Let stand until cool and firm. Break into pieces. Yield: 8 servings.

Shiela Hanley
Carson City, Nevada

DREAM BALLS

1/2 c. margarine
3/4 c. sugar
1 pkg. dates, chopped
2 egg yolks, beaten
1 c. chopped pecans
2 tbsp. marshmallow creme
1 tsp. vanilla
2 c. oven-toasted rice cereal
Powdered sugar or flaked coconut

Combine margarine, sugar, dates, egg yolks, pecans and marshmallow creme in large heavy skillet. Cook over low heat for about 10 minutes, stirring frequently. Remove from heat; stir in vanilla and cereal. Mix well; shape mixture into balls. Roll balls in powdered sugar.

Sarah Elizabeth Yarbrough
Hattiesburg, Mississippi

MICROWAVE CANDY SECRETS

Chocolate melts very easily in the microwave. Break large pieces into a glass bowl and Microwave on Medium-High for 2 to 3 minutes, stirring once. You can use a conventional candy thermometer, be sure to remove it from the candy before returning it to the microwave.

Inez Finegan
Virginia Beach, Virginia

BROWNIES

1/2 c. margarine
1 c. sugar
2 eggs
3/4 c. flour
3 tbsp. cocoa
6 tbsp. cream
Pinch of salt
1 tsp. vanilla
1 c. chopped nuts

Cream margarine and sugar; beat in eggs. Add flour, cocoa, cream, salt and vanilla; mix until smooth. Stir in nuts. Turn batter into greased pan. Bake at 350 degrees for 25 minutes.

Mrs. Frances Detmer
Weeping Water, Nebraska

MICROWAVE CHUNKY MINI CHIP COOKIES

2/3 c. butter, softened
1 c. packed brown sugar
1 egg
1 tsp. vanilla
1 1/2 c. flour
1/2 tsp. soda
1 1/4 c. oats
1/2 c. raisins
1/2 c. unsalted peanuts
3/4 c. miniature semisweet chocolate chips

Cream butter and brown sugar in mixer bowl until light and fluffy. Beat in egg and vanilla. Add flour, soda and oats; mix well. Stir in raisins, peanuts and chocolate chips. Shape into 1-inch balls. Place 8 balls at a time 2 inches apart in circle on waxed paper-covered plate. Microwave on High for 1 to 1 1/2 minutes or until cookies are firm but slightly moist; do not overcook. Let stand for 10 minutes. Remove to wire rack to complete cooling. Yield: 4 dozen.

Patricia Pruett
Savannah, Georgia

LEMONADE COOKIES

6 6-oz. cans frozen lemonade
1 c. butter
1 1/4 c. sugar
2 eggs
1 tsp. soda
3 c. sifted flour

Thaw lemonade. Cream butter and 1 cup sugar; beat in eggs. Sift soda and flour together; add to creamed mixture alternately with 1/2 cup lemonade. Mix well. Drop batter from teaspoon about 2 inches apart onto greased baking sheets. Bake at 400 degrees for 8 minutes or until cookie edges are lightly browned. Brush cookies with remaining lemonade; sprinkle with remaining sugar. Cool on wire racks. Yield: 6 dozen cookies.

Mrs. Shirley S. Allen
Detroit, Michigan

SOUR CREAM COOKIES

1/2 c. butter
1 c. sugar
1 egg
1/2 c. sour cream
1 tsp. vanilla
2 1/2 c. sifted flour
1/4 tsp. salt
1 tsp. soda
1 tsp. baking powder
1/2 tsp. nutmeg
Cinnamon-sugar

Cream butter and sugar together; add egg, beating well. Add sour cream and vanilla; beat until blended. Sift dry ingredients except cinnamon-sugar together; stir into creamed mixture. Chill dough for 1 hour. Drop dough from tip of spoon onto greased baking sheets, spacing 3 inches apart. Top each cookie with cinnamon-sugar. Bake for about 10 minutes at 350 degrees.

Margaret F. Shanahan
Mamaroneck, New York

MICROWAVE HINTS FOR COOKIES

You can make your own microwave cookie sheet by covering a piece of cardboard with waxed paper. It is not necessary to grease the dish for bar cookies. If you do grease the dish, do not sprinkle it with flour. The combination of grease and flour forms a sticky layer on the bottom.

Sally Pederson
Carbondale, Illinois

REFRIGERATOR COOKIE DOUGH TRICK

A wire cheese slicer will cut a roll of chilled cookie dough into cookies of any thickness without breaking or sticking.

Mary Edith King
Gregory, South Dakota

SUGAR COOKIES

1 1/2 c. margarine
4 c. sugar
4 eggs
2 tbsp. cream
4 c. flour
1/8 tsp. salt
4 tsp. baking powder
2 tsp. vanilla
1/2 c. milk
Red food coloring

Cream 1 cup margarine and 2 cups sugar together; add eggs, one at a time, beating well after each addition. Stir in cream. Sift flour with salt and baking powder. Add to creamed mixture; mix well. Stir in 1 teaspoon vanilla. Chill for 20 minutes. Roll out very thin on floured surface; cut with cookie cutter. Place on greased cookie sheet. Bake at 400 degrees until brown. Combine remaining sugar, milk and remaining margarine in saucepan; bring to a boil. Cook to soft-ball stage. Remove from heat; add food coloring and remaining vanilla; cool. Glaze cooled cookies.

Judy Kelso
Hickman, Kentucky

COOKIE KISSES

2 egg whites
1 c. light brown sugar
2 tbsp. flour
1 tsp. vanilla
2 c. chopped nuts

Beat egg whites until stiff; add brown sugar and flour gradually. Add vanilla; fold in nuts. Drop by spoonfuls, well apart, on greased baking sheet. Bake at 250 degrees for 35 to 40 minutes.

Katherine M. Simons
Cross, South Carolina

CHERRY-TOPPED MERINGUE

6 egg whites
3/4 tsp. cream of tartar
2 c. sugar
2 c. soda crackers, crumbled
3/4 c. chopped nuts
2 tsp. vanilla
1/2 pt. whipping cream, whipped
1 can cherry pie filling

Beat egg whites with cream of tartar until frothy; add sugar gradually, beating until stiff. Fold in crumbs; fold in nuts and vanilla. Spread in oblong baking dish. Bake for 25 minutes at 350 degrees. Cool. Cover with whipped cream; spread pie filling over top. Refrigerate overnight. Cut into squares to serve. Yield: 10 servings.

Lorene English
Norcross, Georgia

BLACK FOREST TORTE

4 oz. unsweetened chocolate
1 3/4 c. flour
Sugar
1 1/4 tsp. soda
1/4 tsp. baking powder
1 tsp. salt
2 tsp. vanilla
Soft margarine
3 eggs
1 1/2 4-oz. bars sweet cooking chocolate
1/2 c. chopped toasted almonds
2 c. whipping cream

Melt unsweetened chocolate in double boiler; cool. Combine flour, 1 3/4 cups sugar, 1 1/4 cups water, soda, baking powder, salt, 1 teaspoon vanilla, 2/3 cup margarine and melted chocolate in large electric mixer bowl. Beat at low speed to blend. Beat for 2 minutes at medium speed, scraping side of bowl frequently. Add eggs; beat for 2 minutes longer. Pour 1/4 of the batter into each of 4 greased 9-inch layer cake pans. Bake at 350 degrees for 15 to 18 minutes or until cakes test done. Cool slightly; remove from pans. Cool well. Melt sweet chocolate in double boiler; cool. Blend in 3/4 cup margarine and almonds. Beat cream until stiff, adding 1 tablespoon sugar and remaining vanilla. Alternate chocolate mixture and whipped cream between cake layers, ending with chocolate mixture on top.

Janice Brown
Imperial, Nebraska

APPLE PIE

5 apples, sliced
1 1/2 c. sugar
1/8 tsp. salt
1/2 tsp. cinnamon
Flour
3 tbsp. water
1 unbaked pastry shell
1/2 c. margarine

Combine apples, 1 cup sugar, salt, cinnamon, 1/3 cup flour and water; mix well. Spoon apple mixture into pastry shell. Combine remaining sugar and 1/2 cup flour; cut in margarine until crumbly. Spread crumbs over apple mixture. Place pie in paper bag. Fold ends of bag closed; fasten with paper clips. Place on baking sheet. Bake at 425 degrees for 1 hour.

Mrs. Angeline Boehnke
Flatonia, Texas

BOWL-OVER APPLE PIE

5 c. canned apple slices
1/2 c. water
1/2 to 3/4 c. brown sugar
Dash of salt
2 tbsp. butter or margarine
1 tbsp. grated lemon rind
Pastry for 1-crust pie
Nutmeg

Combine all ingredients except pastry and nutmeg in saucepan; cook over moderate heat until hot and thickened. Roll out pastry into a 12-inch round; prick all over. Place a round bottomed heatproof bowl or casserole on cookie sheet or double thickness of heavy foil; press pastry lightly to bowl. Turn back overhang flush with edge of bowl to make double edge flute or press with fork. Bake in 400-degree oven for about 12 to 14 minutes or until browned and crisp. Cool for several minutes; carefully lift pastry crust from bowl. Place like a bowl on serving dish. Spoon hot apple filling into crust; sprinkle generously with nutmeg. Serve at once with whipped cream or ice cream.

Photograph for this recipe on page 2.

BLACK BOTTOM PIE

18 chocolate wafers, crushed
1/2 c. sugar
1/4 c. melted butter
1 6-oz. package chocolate chips
1/2 c. heavy cream
1/2 tsp. vanilla
1/2 pt. chocolate ice cream, softened
1 qt. orange sherbet, softened

Combine first 3 ingredients; mix well. Press into 9-inch pie plate. Chill. Cook chocolate chips and cream over low heat, stirring occasionally, until melted. Stir in vanilla; chill until thickened. Spoon chocolate ice cream into crust. Spread 3/4 of the chocolate sauce over ice cream; freeze until firm. Spoon sherbet over chocolate sauce. Drizzle remaining chocolate sauce on top. Freeze until firm.

Mrs. Deborah Wheeler
Cabot, Vermont

BUTTERSCOTCH BANANA PIE

2 c. milk
2/3 c. (packed) light brown sugar
1/3 c. flour
3/4 tsp. salt
3 eggs, slightly beaten
2 tsp. butter
1 tsp. vanilla
1 9-in. baked pie shell
3 ripe bananas, sliced

Scald milk in heavy saucepan. Combine and mix brown sugar, flour and salt. Stir into milk slowly. Cook, stirring constantly, for about 10 minutes or until thick. Stir small amount of hot mixture into beaten eggs; stir egg mixture into hot mixture. Cook for 1 minute. Remove from heat; stir in butter and vanilla completing butterscotch filling. Cool thoroughly. Cover bottom of pie shell with small amount of filling. Add alternate layers of sliced bananas and butterscotch filling, ending with filling. Chill. Serve with sweetened whipped cream and additional banana slices if desired.

BUTTERMILK PIE

1 c. sugar
3 tbsp. flour
2 eggs, beaten
1/2 c. melted margarine
1 c. buttermilk
2 tsp. vanilla
1 tsp. lemon flavoring
1 unbaked pastry shell

Combine sugar and flour; add eggs, margarine, buttermilk and flavorings. Mix well; turn into pastry shell. Bake at 425 degrees for 10 minutes. Reduce oven temperature to 350 degrees; bake for 30 minutes longer.

Mrs. Molly Bedrich
Lancaster, Texas

MICROWAVE CREAMY COCONUT PIE

3/4 c. sugar
6 tbsp. flour
2 eggs
2 c. milk
1 tbsp. butter
1 tsp. vanilla
1 c. coconut
1 baked 9-in. pie shell

Combine sugar and flour in deep glass bowl. Whisk in eggs and milk until smooth. Microwave on High for 8 minutes, stirring 3 times. Stir in butter and vanilla. Add coconut. Cool for 5 minutes. Pour into pie shell. Chill.

Katy Fordham
Shreveport, Louisiana

MICROWAVED PIE SHELLS

Pastry will be more eye-appealing if you add 1 or 2 drops of yellow food coloring to the water for the pastry or brush the pastry shell with diluted dark corn syrup before microwaving.

Claudia Surratt
Mena, Arkansas

GIRDLE-BUSTER PIE

20 Oreo cookies, crushed
1/4 c. melted butter
1 qt. vanilla ice cream, softened
1 sm. can evaporated milk

2 tbsp. butter
1/2 c. sugar
2 sq. bitter chocolate
1/2 tsp. vanilla
Whipped cream
Toasted slivered almonds

Combine cookie crumbs and butter; press into pie pan. Freeze. Spoon in ice cream. Freeze until serving time. Combine milk, butter, sugar, chocolate and vanilla in saucepan. Cook over low heat until sauce is smooth, stirring frequently; cool. Serve pie topped with sauce, whipped cream and slivered almonds.

Mrs. Sara Martin Conkle
Chelsea, Alabama

FROZEN LEMON SHERBET PIE

1 pkg. Nabisco wafers, crushed
3 eggs, separated
Juice of 1 lemon
2 tsp. lemon rind
1/2 c. whipping cream, whipped
3/4 c. sugar

Press layer of wafer crumbs in well-buttered 9-inch pie pan, reserving some for topping. Beat egg yolks until thick; stir in lemon juice, rind and whipped cream. Beat egg whites until soft peaks form; add sugar gradually, beating constantly until stiff peaks form. Fold into egg yolk mixture; pour over crust. Top with reserved crumbs. Freeze until firm. Let pie soften slightly before serving. Yield: 6-8 servings.

Judith A. Evans
Wamsutter, Wyoming

HEAVENLY LEMON PIE

2 eggs, separated
Sugar
1 tsp. vanilla
1/2 tsp. vinegar
2 tbsp. cornstarch
1 c. warm water
1 tbsp. grated lemon rind
3 tbsp. lemon juice
1 c. cream

Beat egg whites until soft peaks form. Add 1/2 cup sugar gradually, 2 tablespoons at a time, beating for 2 minutes after each addition. Add vanilla and vinegar. Beat at high speed until stiff peaks form. Spread on bottom and side of greased 9-inch pie plate; shape hollow in center. Bake at 275 degrees for 50 to 60 minutes, until light brown. Combine 1/2 cup sugar, cornstarch and water in double boiler. Cook, for 8 to 10 minutes, stirring, until thickened and clear. Spoon small amount hot mixture into beaten egg yolks; return to double boiler. Add lemon rind and lemon juice. Cook, stirring, for 2 minutes longer. Remove from heat; cover and cool. Whip cream until thick; fold in 2 tablespoons sugar. Place whipped cream in meringue crust; spoon cooled lemon filling over cream. Refrigerate for 8 to 12 hours before serving. May combine lemon filling with whipped cream before placing in crust if desired. Yield: 6 servings.

Eileen S. Brenden
Mahnomen, Minnesota

MACAROON PIE

3 egg whites
3/4 c. sugar
1 tsp. almond flavoring
12 saltine crackers, crushed
12 dates, chopped
1/2 c. chopped nuts
Whipped cream

Beat egg whites until soft peaks form; add sugar gradually. Beat until stiff peaks form. Add flavoring. Combine crackers, dates and nuts; fold into egg white mixture. Place cracker mixture in greased 10-inch pie pan. Bake for 30 to 35 minutes at 325 degrees. Serve with whipped cream or whipped topping. Yield: 6-8 servings.

Judith W. Arnold
Glenshaw, Pennsylvania

HOW TO IMPROVE PIE PASTRY

Add 1 teaspoon vinegar to cold water in preparing pie pastry for flakier pie crusts.

Beatrice Campbell
Leland, Mississippi

MILE HIGH LEMON PIE

1 env. unflavored gelatin
1 1/2 c. sugar
1/2 c. lemon juice
1/2 tsp. salt
4 eggs, separated
1 tsp. grated lemon rind
1 baked 9-in. crumb crust
1/2 c. whipping cream, whipped

Soften gelatin in 1/4 cup cold water in mixing bowl. Combine 1 cup sugar, lemon juice and salt in top of double boiler; mix. Stir in beaten egg yolks; cook, stirring constantly, until thickened. Add to gelatin, stirring until gelatin is dissolved; stir in lemon rind. Chill until partially set. Beat egg whites until stiff; beat in remaining sugar gradually. Fold into lemon mixture. Spoon lightly into crumb crust, piling high. Chill for several hours. Top with whipped cream.

Sister Mary Louise
Clarksburg, West Virginia

MICROWAVE PECAN PIE

1 unbaked 9-in. pie shell
Dried beans
1/4 c. butter
1 tbsp. flour
3 eggs, beaten
1 c. dark corn syrup
2/3 c. sugar
1/2 tsp. vanilla
1 c. pecan halves

Line pie shell with plastic wrap. Fill to depth of 1 inch with dried beans. Microwave on Medium for 8 minutes, turning once. Remove plastic wrap and beans. Microwave for 3 minutes longer. Microwave butter in glass dish on High for 1 minute. Blend in flour. Cool slightly. Add eggs, corn syrup and sugar; mix well. Microwave on Medium for 10 minutes or until slightly thickened, stirring occasionally. Stir in vanilla. Pour into pie shell. Arrange pecans on top. Microwave on Medium-Low for 8 minutes or just until set, turning once. Yield: 8 servings.

Theresa Benson
Ryan, Oklahoma

PEACH-PECAN PIE

3 eggs, beaten
1 No. 2 can peach pie filling
1/4 tsp. salt
1 c. dark corn syrup
1 c. pecan halves
1 tsp. vanilla
1 10-in. unbaked pie shell

Combine eggs, pie filling and salt. Add corn syrup, pecans and vanilla. Pour into pie shell. Bake at 425 degrees for 10 minutes; reduce oven temperature to 325 degrees. Bake for 45 to 50 minutes longer or until set.

NEW FLAVOR FOR APPLE PIE

Apple pie will have a new flavor if a small amount of grated orange rind is added to sugar and sprinkled over the apples. Grated cheese may be sprinkled over pie pastry and rolled into the pastry for a different and delicious change in crust.

Mrs. Nadine Kaiser
Hydro, Oklahoma

PECAN TASSIES

1 3-oz. package cream cheese, softened
Softened margarine
1 c. sifted flour
1 egg, lightly beaten
3/4 c. (firmly packed) brown sugar

1 tsp. vanilla
Dash of salt
2/3 c. chopped pecans

Blend cream cheese with 1/2 cup margarine until smooth. Add flour; blend well. Chill for 2 hours or longer. Shape dough into twenty-four 1-inch balls; press into 1 3/4-inch muffin cups. Blend egg, brown sugar, vanilla, 1 teaspoon margarine, salt and pecans in small bowl; fill pastry cups. Bake at 375 degrees for 20 minutes or until lightly browned.

Mrs. Paula Calhoun
Fisher, Illinois

TRADITIONAL PUMPKIN PIE

1 1/2 c. pumpkin
1 1/2 c. brown sugar
1/2 tsp. salt
1 tsp. ginger
1/4 tsp. allspice
3 tbsp. molasses
3 lge. eggs
1 c. milk
1 unbaked 9-in. pie shell

Combine all ingredients except pie shell; mix well. Turn into pie shell. Bake at 375 degrees for 55 minutes to 1 hour or until firm.

Mrs. Maril Singleton
Princeton, New Jersey

MICROWAVE APPLE CRISP

4 c. sliced apples
1/2 c. oats
1/4 c. flour
1/4 c. packed brown sugar
1/4 c. butter
1 tsp. lemon juice
1/2 tsp. cinnamon
1/8 tsp. nutmeg

Place apples in 8 x 8-inch glass dish. Combine oats, flour, brown sugar, butter, lemon juice and spices in bowl; mix well. Sprinkle over apples. Microwave, covered, on High for 8 to 10 minutes or until apples are tender. Serve warm or cool.

Rosalie Goff
Glenrock, Wyoming

LUSCIOUS BANANA PUDDING

1/4 c. cornstarch
1 c. sugar
1/4 tsp. salt
2 c. milk
3 eggs, separated
2 tbsp. butter
1/2 tsp. vanilla
1 pkg. vanilla wafers
1 lb. bananas, sliced

Blend cornstarch, 2/3 cup sugar and salt together well; stir in milk gradually. Cook in double boiler for about 10 minutes or until thickened, stirring constantly. Stir small amount of hot mixture gradually into lightly beaten egg yolks; stir into remaining hot mixture. Cook for 5 minutes, stirring constantly; remove from heat. Add butter and vanilla; mix well. Cool. Arrange alternate layers of vanilla wafers, bananas and egg mixture in baking dish. Beat egg whites until foamy; beat in remaining sugar gradually, beating meringue until stiff. Spread over pudding. Bake in 450-degree oven for about 5 minutes or until lightly browned.

Mrs. Frances J. Jacox
Halls, Tennessee

FAMILY RICE PUDDING

2 qt. milk
1 c. sugar
1 c. rice
Pinch of salt
1 tsp. vanilla

Combine all ingredients in baking dish; stir lightly. Bake in 325-degree oven for 1 hour or until rice is tender, stirring twice.

Barbara Newton
Hudson Falls, New York

FRESH FRUIT PANCAKES

1 pt. strawberries, sliced
1 c. fresh blueberries
Sugar
2 c. complete pancake mix
1 1/3 c. water
Melted butter
Sour cream
Brown sugar

Mix strawberries and blueberries; sprinkle lightly with sugar. Mix pancake mix and water until fairly smooth. Spoon batter onto hot, lightly greased griddle; turn pancakes when edges look cooked. Brush with butter. Stack 2 or 3 pancakes on each plate; top with fruit and a dollop of sour cream. Sprinkle with brown sugar.

Felicia Brubaker
El Cajon, California

PEACH-BUTTERSCOTCH SURPRISE

1 c. flour
1/8 tsp. salt
Nonfat dry milk
1/3 c. shortening
1/4 c. sugar
2 1/2 c. sliced fresh peaches
1 pkg. butterscotch instant pudding mix
2 egg whites
1/4 c. light brown sugar
1/2 tsp. vanilla

Sift flour, salt and 2 tablespoons dry milk together. Cut in shortening until consistency of cornmeal. Add 3 tablespoons water gradually until mixture clings together. Roll on lightly floured board to 12 x 12-inch square. Fit into 9-inch square pan, bringing up on sides. Flute edges. Sprinkle with half the sugar. Spread with peaches. Sprinkle with remaining sugar. Cover with aluminum foil. Bake at 350 degrees for 45 minutes. Remove foil; bake until edges are brown. Remove from oven. Combine pudding mix with 1/2 cup dry milk; add 2 cups water. Beat until smooth. Pour over peaches. Beat egg whites until very stiff. Add brown sugar gradually, mixing thoroughly. Add vanilla. Spread meringue over top, sealing edges. Return to oven for about 15 minutes or until brown.

PEACH-GRAHAM CRUMBLE

1 No. 2 1/2 can sliced peaches
1/2 c. graham cracker crumbs
1/3 c. (packed) brown sugar
1/2 tsp. cinnamon
3 tbsp. soft butter or margarine

Drain peaches; cut slices into chunks. Spread in 8 or 9-inch pie pan. Blend remaining ingredients until crumbly; sprinkle over peaches. Bake at 375 degrees for 35 minutes. Serve warm with cream or ice cream if desired. Yield: 4 servings.

Barbara Daugherty
Torrance, California

OLD-FASHIONED ICE CREAM

6 eggs
2 c. sugar
2 qt. whipping cream
2 tbsp. vanilla
1 qt. (about) milk

Beat eggs; add sugar, beating until creamy. Stir in whipping cream and vanilla. Pour into 1-gallon container of hand-turned style ice cream freezer; fill container with milk to within 3 or 4 inches from top. Cover. Place in freezer bucket; fill bucket with alternate layers of crushed ice and half the ice amount of ice cream salt. Freeze according to freezer directions.

Mrs. R. Gale Manley
Bristol, Virginia

FROZEN PINEAPPLE MOUSSE

1 9-oz. can crushed pineapple
3 eggs, separated
Dash of salt
5/8 c. sugar
2 tbsp. lemon juice
1 c. heavy cream, whipped
2 c. vanilla wafer crumbs

Drain pineapple; reserve juice. Beat egg yolks, beating in salt and 1/2 cup sugar. Blend in reserved pineapple juice and lemon juice. Cook in double boiler, stirring constantly, until mixture coats spoon; stir in pineapple. Cool. Beat egg whites until stiff; beat in remaining sugar gradually. Fold egg whites and whipped cream into pineapple mixture. Line 2 ice cube trays with half the crumbs; spread whipped cream mixture over crumbs. Sprinkle with remaining crumbs. Freeze. Yield: 8 servings.

Mrs. John R. Bell
Coon Rapids, Minnesota

MICROWAVE TOASTED ALMONDS

Toasted buttered almonds are a snap to make in the microwave. Microwave 2 tablespoons butter on High in a 9-inch glass pie plate for 45 seconds to 1 minute or until melted. Stir in 1/4 cup slivered almonds. Microwave for 3 to 4 minutes. Let stand for 2 minutes. Sprinkle on ice cream or other favorite desserts.

Marilyn Gerrard
Cullman, Alabama

MICROWAVE FRUITED PUDDING

1 16-oz. can sliced peaches
1 16-oz. can pineapple chunks
1 11-oz. can mandarin oranges
1 3-oz. package vanilla pudding and pie filling mix
1 3-oz. package tapioca pudding mix

Drain fruits, reserving juices. Add enough water to reserved juices to measure 3 cups. Combine juice with pudding mix and tapioca mix in glass dish; mix well. Microwave on High for 6 minutes or until thickened and clear, stirring once. Microwave for 3 minutes longer. Cool. Stir in fruit. Chill until serving time. Yield: 10 servings.

Linda Nelson
New Hampton, Iowa

MICROWAVE BAKED APPLES

Bake apples in record time in your microwave. Fill the cores with your favorite ingredients and place them in a glass dish. Microwave 1 apple on High for 2 to 3 minutes; microwave 2 apples for 4 to 6 minutes; microwave 4 apples for 8 to 10 minutes. Apples will still be somewhat firm at the end of the cooking time but will continue to cook during the standing time.

Bessie Tolliver
Boulder, Colorado

Equivalent Chart

	WHEN RECIPE CALLS FOR:	YOU NEED:
BREAD & CEREAL	1 c. soft bread crumbs	2 slices
	1 c. fine dry bread crumbs	4-5 slices
	1 c. small bread cubes	2 slices
	1 c. fine cracker crumbs	24 saltines
	1 c. fine graham cracker crumbs	14 crackers
	1 c. vanilla wafer crumbs	22 wafers
	1 c. crushed corn flakes	3 c. uncrushed
	4 c. cooked macaroni	1 8-oz. package
	3 1/2 c. cooked rice	1 c. uncooked
DAIRY	1 c. freshly grated cheese	1/4 lb.
	1 c. cottage cheese or sour cream	1 8-oz. carton
	2/3 c. evaporated milk	1 sm. can
	1 2/3 c. evaporated milk	1 tall can
	1 c. whipped cream	1/2 c. heavy cream
SWEET	1 c. semisweet chocolate pieces	1 6-oz. package
	2 c. granulated sugar	1 lb.
	4 c. sifted confectioners' sugar	1 lb.
	2 1/4 c. packed brown sugar	1 lb.
MEAT	3 c. diced cooked meat	1 lb., cooked
	2 c. ground cooked meat	1 lb., cooked
	4 c. diced cooked chicken	1 5-lb. chicken
NUTS	1 c. chopped nuts	4 oz. shelled 1 lb. unshelled
FRUIT	4 c. sliced or chopped apples	4 medium
	2 c. pitted cherries	4 c. unpitted
	3 to 4 tbsp. lemon juice plus 1 tsp. grated peel	1 lemon
	1/3 c. orange juice plus 2 tsp. grated peel	1 orange
	1 c. mashed banana	3 medium
	4 c. cranberries	1 lb.
	3 c. shredded coconut	1/2 lb.
	4 c. sliced peaches	8 medium
	1 c. pitted dates or candied fruit	1 8-oz. package
	2 c. pitted prunes	1 12-oz. package
	3 c. raisins	1 15-oz. package

	WHEN RECIPE CALLS FOR:	YOU NEED:
VEGETABLES	4 c. sliced or diced raw potatoes	4 medium
	2 c. cooked green beans	1/2 lb. fresh or 1 16-oz. can
	1 c. chopped onion	1 large
	4 c. shredded cabbage	1 lb.
	2 c. canned tomatoes	1 16-oz. can
	1 c. grated carrot	1 large
	2 1/2 c. lima beans or red beans	1 c. dried, cooked
	1 4-oz. can mushrooms	1/2 lb. fresh

COMMON EQUIVALENTS

1 tbsp. = 3 tsp.	4 qt. = 1 gal.
2 tbsp. = 1 oz.	6 1/2 to 8-oz. can = 1 c.
4 tbsp. = 1/4 c.	10 1/2 to 12-oz. can = 1 1/4 c.
5 tbsp. + 1 tsp. = 1/3 c.	14 to 16-oz. can (No. 300) = 1 3/4 c.
8 tbsp. = 1/2 c.	16 to 17-oz. can (No. 303) = 2 c.
12 tbsp. = 3/4 c.	1-lb. 4-oz. can or 1-pt. 2-oz. can (No. 2) = 2 1/2 c.
16 tbsp. = 1 c.	1-lb. 13-oz. can (No. 2 1/2) = 3 1/2 c.
1 c. = 8 oz. or 1/2 pt.	3-lb. 3-oz. can or 46-oz. can or 1-qt. 14-oz. can = 5 3/4 c.
4 c. = 1 qt.	6 1/2-lb. or 7-lb. 5-oz. can (No. 10) = 12 to 13 c.

Metric Conversion Chart

VOLUME

1 tsp.	=	4.9 cc
1 tbsp.	=	14.7 cc
1/3 c.	=	28.9 cc
1/8 c.	=	29.5 cc
1/4 c.	=	59.1 cc
1/2 c.	=	118.3 cc
3/4 c.	=	177.5 cc
1 c.	=	236.7 cc
2 c.	=	473.4 cc
1 fl. oz.	=	29.5 cc
4 oz.	=	118.3 cc
8 oz.	=	236.7 cc
1 pt.	=	473.4 cc
1 qt.	=	.946 liters
1 gal.	=	3.7 liters

CONVERSION FACTORS

Liters	X	1.056	=	Liquid quarts
Quarts	X	0.946	=	Liters
Liters	X	0.264	=	Gallons
Gallons	X	3.785	=	Liters
Fluid ounces	X	29.563	=	Cubic centimeters
Cubic centimeters	X	0.034	=	Fluid ounces
Cups	X	236.575	=	Cubic centimeters
Tablespoons	X	14.797	=	Cubic centimeters
Teaspoons	X	4.932	=	Cubic centimeters
Bushels	X	0.352	=	Hectoliters
Hectoliters	X	2.837	=	Bushels

WEIGHT

1 dry oz.	=	28.3 Grams
1 lb.	=	.454 Kilograms

CONVERSION FACTORS:

Ounces (Avoir.)	X	28.349	=	Grams
Grams	X	0.035	=	Ounces
Pounds	X	0.454	=	Kilograms
Kilograms	X	2.205	=	Pounds

Index

Microwave recipe page numbers are preceded by M.

MICROWAVE COOKING TIPS

MONEY-SAVING IDEAS

PHOTOGRAPHY CREDITS: General Foods Kitchens; American Home Foods; Best Foods; A Division of Corn Products Company, Inc.; California Raisin Advisory Board; Processed Apples Institute; McIlhenny Company; Anderson, Clayton and Company: Chiffon Margarine; American Mushroom Institute; Keith Thomas Company; Pie Filling Institute; Evaporated Milk Association; National Kraut Packers Association; National Macaroni Institute; U. S. Department of Commerce: National Marine Fisheries Service; Diamond Walnut Kitchen; American Dairy Association; American Dry Milk Institute; National Fisheries Institute; Cling Peach Advisory Board; National Dairy Association; Frozen Potato Products Institute.